PAUL

Man on a Mission

Other books by Bob Hartman and Conrad Gempf

Bob Hartman (published by Lion Children's)
The Lion Storyteller Bible
The Lion Storyteller Awesome Book of Stories
Old Testament Tales: The Unauthorized Version
New Testament Tales: The Unauthorized Version
Off the Wall Bible Tales

Conrad Gempf
Jesus Asked: Zondervan
Mealtime Habits of the Messiah: Zondervan
How to Like Paul Again: Authentic
New Bible Commentary (contributor): IVP
Dictionary of Paul and his Letters (contributor): IVP
Consultant to the NIV translation committee

PAUL

Man on a Mission

Bob Hartman and Conrad Gempf
Illustrated by Dave Smith

LION
CHILDREN'S

For Sam and Sara Hargreaves, who suggested the idea;
and for Peter Oakes, whose work showed the way.

Published by
Lion Children's Books
an imprint of
Lion Hudson IP Ltd
Wilkinson House, Jordan Hill Road,
Oxford OX2 8DR, England
www.lionhudson.com/lionchildrens

ISBN 978 0 7459 7739 3

First edition 2017

Acknowledgments
Scripture quotations are the authors' own interpretation.

A catalogue record for this book is available from the British Library

Printed and bound in the UK, September 2017, LH26

CONTENTS

CHAPTER 1

AN AMBITIOUS STUDENT

ACTS 5:34FF ▦ GALATIANS 1:13–14

My friends, hello! I'm glad you came! Welcome to the library – mind you don't trip over that pile of scrolls. My name is Max (short for Maximus), and here on my shelves I have all sorts of scrolls about all sorts of subjects.

I think you wanted to know about Paul? Over on this shelf you'll find stories about Paul, written by his friend Luke, in a set of scrolls called The Acts of the Apostles. No, I said "Acts"! They didn't actually use axes much. Although at one point I can imagine… but we'll talk about that later.

Now, on this shelf, you'll find the scrolls that were written by Paul himself, long letters to some of his friends, the ones that Luke describes him meeting in the Acts scrolls. So, between the letters that Paul wrote and all that Luke wrote about him and his adventures, you'll be able to find out everything you want to know.

Don't worry, I know there's an awful lot of material to look through, but I can "show you around" through the various letters if you like.

You know, when the whole thing started, Paul wan't even called Paul. At first, he was called Saul. He was a Jewish man, just as Jesus was a Jewish man. But at first, instead of telling people about Jesus, Saul thought Jesus was horrible. And he thought that people who believed in Jesus were making a big mistake.

Once, when Paul was thinking back to those days, he wrote to his friends in Galatia:

"I know that you have heard me tell about how I used to live. I tried to hurt the people who followed Jesus and tried to break up their group."

(GALATIANS 1:13)

Not all the people in the Jewish religion felt this way, though. Even some who didn't follow Jesus themselves tried to get along with those who did. They thought the Jesus stuff would just fade away. The funny thing is that Saul's own teacher thought that way! Luke tells his story in Acts:

It all began with a prison visit.

Saul. His teacher, Gamaliel. And the Jewish Council of Leaders that Gamaliel belonged to and all the people they had put in jail were all Jewish.

Why had they been put in jail? Because those people would not stop talking about Jesus, who was also Jewish, as it happens.

You see, the people in prison were followers of Jesus. In fact, they were the leaders of Jesus' followers – his apostles. They had watched him die, and then seen him and talked with him and even eaten with him, after he had come back to life. Then they had stared, amazed, as he rose into the clouds to join God in heaven.

Is it any wonder that they wanted to share this good news with everyone else? And more to the point, is it any wonder that they were convinced that Jesus was the long-awaited saviour – the Messiah – that God had promised to send to his people?

The Jewish leaders, however, were not convinced. They thought that all this talk about Jesus was leading the Jewish people astray, passing on things that were not true, and maybe even giving the people the false hope that they could overthrow the Romans who had conquered their land.

Time and time again they had warned the apostles to stop talking about Jesus. But the apostles would not stop. So the Jewish leaders arrested them and put them in prison.

And that brings us to the prison visitor.

The prison visitor was not a man with comforting words to encourage them while they were behind bars.

As a matter of fact, the prison visitor was not a man, at all. No, the prison visitor was an angel!

The angel opened the prison door. He led the apostles out. Then he told them to go to the Temple and carry on telling everyone about Jesus. And that's exactly what they were doing as the sun rose the next morning.

At about the same time, the Jewish leaders said to their officers, "Bring us the prisoners."

The officers went to the prison, as ordered. But they returned with the strangest story:

"The prison doors were locked," they said. "The guards were standing to attention. But when we went in, the prison cells were empty!"

Now if anyone ever tells you that God does not have a sense of humour, you simply need to let them in on this next amazing bit of comic timing. For as soon as the officers had told the Jewish leaders that the prisoners had somehow disappeared, a messenger rushed into the room, shouting, "You know those men you threw into prison for talking about Jesus? They're in the Temple courts, right now, as we speak. Talking about Jesus!"

The officers went to the Temple courts and escorted the apostles back to the Jewish leaders. But they didn't arrest them this time, and they didn't use force, because the people who were listening seemed to like what they were hearing. And the officers didn't want to upset them.

"We told you to stop talking about Jesus!" the Jewish leaders said to the apostles. "But here you are, doing the exact opposite. And what's more, you're blaming us for his death. This has got to stop!"

Peter, the leader of the apostles, spoke for them all.

"We have a duty to obey what God tells us to do," he explained. "Not what men tell us.

"And we know, because we have seen it, that God brought Jesus back to life. That's right, the same Jesus you crucified. What's more, Jesus really is the Messiah that God promised to send, who is in heaven, now, with God – offering forgiveness to all our people. And we know this because God's own Holy Spirit has made it clear to us."

As they listened to Peter's speech, the Jewish leaders grew more and more angry. They disagreed with everything he said. And by the time he was finished, they had decided to kill him and the other apostles to put an end to their teaching.

And that's when Gamaliel stood up. He was a Pharisee, which meant he was very keen to keep all the Jewish laws. In fact, he knew so much about the Jewish law that he taught others, including Saul, of course.

Gamaliel could feel the temperature rising in the room. He understood how upset the other Jewish leaders were. But he had a different solution to the problem that faced them.

"Send these men out of the room," he ordered. And when the apostles had gone, he addressed his fellow leaders.

"We have seen 'movements' like this before," he said. "There was Theudas, for example, who, like Jesus, thought that he was someone special. He had, what, four hundred followers? But when he was killed, his followers gave up and it all came to nothing.

"And then there was that fellow from Galilee – Judas, that's it! He had a following too. But when he died, his movement died with him.

"So I say that we leave these followers of Jesus alone. If what they say about Jesus is just their idea, then their cause will die out on its own.

"But," and here Gamaliel paused for emphasis, "If what they say is true – if it really is from God – then no power on earth will be able to stop them. And we may well find ourselves fighting against God, himself."

The other leaders nodded in agreement. And instead of killing the apostles, they simply had them beaten, and told them, once again, to stop talking about Jesus.

And what did the apostles do, once they had been released? They thanked God. That's right. Because they were happy to be able to do God's work, even if it meant suffering as Jesus had suffered before them.

Then they went out in the streets and went right back to talking about Jesus!

Saul was the smartest student in Gamaliel's class. He wrote to his friends in Galatia:

> "I was ahead of others my age in the study and practice of Judaism. I loved the old ways so much that I worked really hard at following them."
>
> (GALATIANS 1:14)

But Saul did not follow his teacher in everything. The two of them felt very differently about people who followed Jesus. Gamaliel was patient, but Saul...?

CHAPTER 2

THE PERSECUTOR

ACTS 7:60 – 8:4 ▪ 1 CORINTHIANS 15:3–10A

Not all the people were as patient as Gamaliel. And others probably ran out of patience when people kept following Jesus. Saul was one of those who got angry and used force. He became an enemy of Jesus' followers.

Imagine how sorry he was about all this later. After he began following Jesus, he wrote about it to friends of his in the city of Corinth:

"I am the least of the messengers. Maybe I don't even deserve to be one, because I caused such trouble to the church of God back then. It is only by God's gift that I am what I am."

(1 CORINTHIANS 15:9–10a)

Back then, though, Saul had approved of others who fought against those who trusted in Jesus. In fact, he became a leader in seeking out and breaking up groups of Jesus' followers, as you'll see...

Saul was so intent on opposing Jesus that he got involved in a stoning.

What's a stoning? It's when a group of people grab big stones and rocks and throw them at somebody else until that person dies. Pretty nasty, I know.

You see, the followers of Jesus kept on telling people about him, even though the Jewish leaders had told them to stop. And as a result, many more people believed in Jesus – even some of the Jewish priests. And that made the Jewish leaders even more angry.

They were particularly annoyed by a follower of Jesus called Stephen, a good man, filled with God's Holy Spirit. He had been appointed by the apostles to take care of widows and make sure they had enough to eat.

Stephen also performed miracles and, of course, he liked to tell people about Jesus.

One day, while he was talking about Jesus, he got into an argument with some other Jews, who disagreed with what he was saying. With the help of God's Holy Spirit, Stephen was winning the argument, and that frustrated his opponents. So they found some men to tell lies about Stephen and say that he was dishonouring God with the things he taught.

In the end, they dragged Stephen before the Jewish leaders where more lies were told about him.

"He wants to change the laws that Moses gave us," the men lied. "And he says that Jesus of Nazareth will destroy our temple!"

None of this was true, of course. But instead of fighting back, Stephen just fixed his gaze on them: people who were there said he had the look of an angel about him!

Then he talked to the Jewish leaders about the history that they all shared together – the history of God's people, the Jews. He spoke of .Abraham and Joseph. Of Moses and the Exodus. Of King David and King Solomon.

Finally, he spoke of the prophets, God's messengers, and reminded the Jewish leaders that when God sent those prophets, his people often rejected them and sometimes even put them to death.

"And that's what you did to Jesus," Stephen concluded.

"I see Jesus, even now," said Stephen, his eyes trained on heaven. "He's standing there,.at God's side."

And hearing that, their anger burst forth in a fit of murderous rage. They dragged Stephen out of the city, and rock by jagged rock, they stoned him to death.

Stoning a man to death is hard work. So they took off their coats, and laid them, for safekeeping, at the feet of a young Pharisee and expert in the law. A young man who had been a student of Gamaliel himself. A young man named Saul.

Saul did not throw a stone that day. But, like the Jewish leaders, he believed that what Stephen said about Jesus was wrong and that it was leading the Jewish people astray. So he fully agreed with their decision to put Stephen to death.

And it didn't stop there. Following Stephen's death, the Jewish leaders began a great persecution of the followers of Jesus. It was so bad, that, apart from the apostles, most of the followers of Jesus left Jerusalem and found places to hide in other parts of the country.

As for Saul, he joined right in with the persecution. He went from house to house searching for the followers of Jesus. When he found them, he made sure that they were sent to prison – men and women alike.

And it wasn't long before the name "Saul" was feared by Jesus' followers, all across the land.

Later, Saul felt bad about what he'd done. He didn't let it get in the way of what God called him to do though. Instead, he became one of the Jewish followers of Jesus: part of the group he had been so against! And he now spoke well of people who he once thought of as enemies.

To his friends in Corinth, he wrote:

"For I have told you the news that I myself received. Jesus Christ died for our sins as the Bible said he would. He was buried and then was raised back to life on the third day, again as the Bible said. Jesus met with Peter and then all the Twelve. After that he appeared to more than 500 believers at the same time, most of whom are still alive... Then he appeared to James and all the apostles. And last of all, he appeared to me — I almost came too late!"

(1 CORINTHIANS 15:3–8)

But he did get to see Jesus. It was a complete surprise.

CHAPTER 3

A U-TURN

ACTS 9, 22, 26 ▣ PHILIPPIANS 3:5–9, 13A–14

Saul never expected to see Jesus. He was sure that Jesus was dead. He felt sure about a lot of things. At the beginning, all Jesus' followers were Jewish, just like Saul. And Saul was from a proper Jewish family. He had been careful to do all the right ceremonies and studied hard.

To his friends in the city of Philippi, he wrote about it:

"I am from the people of Israel and from the tribe of Benjamin. My parents were Jews and I am a Jew. I am a Pharisee, a group that thinks a lot about the law. I tried to hurt the church because I was so devoted to the old ways. And I was really good at what I did. But although all those things seemed so good then, because of Christ I now think they are worth nothing."

(PHILIPPIANS 3:5b–7)

Let me tell you about a time when Saul tried hard to do what he thought was the right thing. He believed that catching followers of Jesus and throwing them into jail was what God wanted him to do. God, of course, saw things differently.

Now, about that surprise I mentioned. You might think that it was the followers of Jesus who were surprised, when Saul knocked on their doors and arrested them for teaching something that he disagreed with. You might even think, like them, that he was doing that just because he was evil.

But here's the thing. When Saul went from house to house, searching for the followers of Jesus, he truly believed he was doing what God wanted him to do.

When he arrested those people and had them thrown into prison, he thought he was stopping the spread of an idea that would lead other Jewish people astray. He was convinced that these Jews were wrong to say that Jesus had come back to life and that he was the Messiah that God had always promised to send.

Saul was trying his best to do what he thought was right. And that's why he asked for permission to go after the followers of Jesus who had fled from Jerusalem to Damascus, and arrest them.

He went right to the chief priest, and asked for letters of recommendation so no one would have any doubt that his mission had been approved at the highest level. Then off he went, with his helpers, straight for Damascus.

Along the way, however, something happened.
A surprise.

First there was a light, so bright and powerful that it knocked Saul off his feet.

Then there was a voice, coming from the light.

"Saul, Saul," the voice called. "Why are you persecuting me?"

"Who are you, Lord?" Saul asked, his voice shaking, his hands trembling.

And then came the second surprise.

"I am Jesus," the voice replied. "It's me you are persecuting."

And right there and then, Saul realized that he had got things completely wrong. The followers of Jesus – his fellow Jews who believed that Jesus was alive – had been right, all along. The evidence was there, before him.

When Saul had arrested and imprisoned and punished them he had, in effect, punished Jesus himself! And so Saul couldn't help but wonder how Jesus was going to punish him, in return.

The orders didn't sound menacing.

"Get up," said Jesus. "Go into the city. And there you will be told what to do."

When Saul tried to get up, he couldn't see a thing. He was blind!

"Is this just the beginning of my punishment?" he wondered, as his friends lifted him to his feet. And the question never left him, as they led him, helpless, into Damascus, and as he waited for three days, praying, without eating or drinking a thing.

While Saul waited, Jesus appeared, in a vision, to one of his followers who lived in Damascus – a man called Ananias.

"I want you to go to Straight Street," said Jesus. "To the house of a man called Judas. Saul of Tarsus is there, praying, and I have shown him a vision of you, laying your hands on him and taking away his blindness."

Now it was Ananias's turn to be surprised.

"But, Lord," he replied. "Saul of Tarsus has done many evil things to your followers in Jerusalem. And from what I have heard, he means to do the same evil things here! He has letters from the chief priest giving him permission to arrest us and throw us into prison!"

"I have different plans for Saul," said Jesus. "I have chosen him, specifically, to tell not only my fellow Jews about me, but also a world full of people who are not Jewish. It will not be easy, and he will suffer greatly for the thing I have called him to do."

So Ananias went to Straight Street, to the house of Judas, and there he met Saul. And they were both surprised.

Ananias found the man who should have been his enemy blind and in need of prayer, humble, and ready to receive whatever the risen Jesus had in store for him.

And Saul? Saul found a gentle pair of hands laid upon him, the return of his sight, and, instead of punishment, forgiveness for all that he had done.

"Was even the blindness," he wondered, "God's way of helping me 'open my eyes' to the truth of who Jesus really is?"

And so Saul was baptized, and came up out of the waters a new man, a changed man, a different man.

And then, just as soon as he could, he went to the synagogues - the Jewish places of worship - and told everyone who would listen that Jesus of Nazareth was alive, and that he was the Son of God, and the Messiah that every Jew had been waiting for.

"Isn't this Saul, who came to punish the followers of Jesus?" They asked friend and foe alike.

And everyone, absolutely everyone, was surprised!

Everything changed for Saul when Jesus met him on the Damascus Road and told him what God really wanted. He learned that he had the wrong idea about what would please God!

Thinking back on it, he later wrote this:

"It's not only the things I did, I now consider everything worthless next to how wonderful it is to really know Jesus Christ the Lord. For him, I've let everything else go. It's like rubbish. Instead what I want is to belong to Jesus. And that doesn't happen by doing everything a Jewish person is supposed to. Instead it happens by trusting Jesus. Being right with God comes through trusting Jesus. Here's the thing:

like a race, I forget what is behind
me and I strain towards what is ahead of
me. I keep going to win the heavenly prize
that God has called me to win, in Jesus
Christ."

(PHILIPPIANS 3:8-9, 13b-14)

That's how Saul began a new life, serving Jesus and
his followers, the very movement he'd once tried to
exterminate!

CHAPTER 4

THE ENCOURAGER

ACTS 9:23–28; 11:19–26 ▫ GALATIANS 1:22–24; 2:7–9

Saul was happy to have found Jesus, but it was also hard for him in Damascus. The people that once were his friends were disappointed with his change of heart. And the people who might have been new friends – the Jewish followers of Jesus – were still scared of him because he used to be their enemy.

"What if he's only pretending?" they thought.

Later, he wrote this to the Galatians:

"In Israel, the churches didn't know me. They'd only heard that a person who was their enemy is now preaching about Jesus instead! This made them grateful to God. Years later, I went to Jerusalem, this time with Barnabas."

(GALATIANS 1:22-24)

Why I remember the first time Saul met Barnabas – it was after his famous basket escape...

It was all rather confusing. Before long, Saul, the hunter of the followers of Jesus, found he had become the hunted.

Some of Saul's former friends wondered if the time had come to get rid of him. They put guards at every gateway in the city, hoping to arrest him and put him to death for betraying their cause.

Somehow Saul found out about their plot to kill him and realized it was time to move on. And instead of leaving Damascus through one of the gates, he departed by an entirely different route.

His new friends found a hole, high in the wall that surrounded the city. They bundled Saul into what must have been a very strong and very big basket.

Then, during the night, they tied ropes to the basket and lowered him through the hole to the ground outside the city. And, from there, he made his escape.

Saul went straight to Jerusalem. And, when he arrived, he tried to join up with the followers of Jesus who were still there. Understandably, they weren't that thrilled to see him. He'd thrown lots of their friends into jail, after all, and he was the reason that lots of their other friends had fled the city. They simply didn't trust him. And, really, who could blame them?

As I said, however, there were among the followers of Jesus some who were less cautious. One of these was

a man called Barnabas, who became a good friend to Paul. His name meant "encourager", and that's pretty much what he was.

When some of the followers of Jesus needed money, for example, he sold a field that he owned and helped them out. And he was there for Saul too.

He took Saul to meet the apostles and told them what had happened to Saul on the Damascus Road – how he had met Jesus and how his life had changed. Then he told them how Saul had been telling people all about Jesus ever since.

And because the apostles trusted Barnabas, they set aside their suspicions, and trusted Saul, as well.

In no time at all, Saul was out on the streets telling people that Jesus was alive, and that he was the Son of God and God's Messiah. And, in no-time-at-all-and-a-bit, he found himself arguing with people who disagreed with him – Jewish people who believed the very same thing that Saul used to believe. It was all very confusing.

In fact, one group of Jews got so fed up arguing with Saul, that they decided to kill him. Which, to be fair, would have made sense to Saul himself, back when he shared their opinion.

When the followers of Jesus discovered this, however, they helped Saul escape again (without the big basket, this time), and sent him back to his home town, Tarsus.

It was about this time that a very interesting thing happened to Peter, the leader of the apostles. Up to that point, all the followers of Jesus were Jewish. And, because they believed that Jesus was the fulfilment of everything the Jewish people had been waiting for, they only talked to other Jewish people about Jesus.

One day, God spoke to Peter in a vision and told him to talk about Jesus to a man named Cornelius, who was not Jewish. He was what Jewish people called a "Gentile". Cornelius believed what he heard, he was filled with God's Holy Spirit, and he became a follower of Jesus.

And soon, other followers of Jesus were telling Gentiles about him too. There were, for example, some men from Cyprus and Cyrene who went to the city of Antioch and told the Gentiles there about Jesus. Many of them decided to follow Jesus, and when news about this reached Jerusalem, the apostles decided to send Barnabas to see what was going on.

Barnabas was really pleased with what was happening in Antioch. He encouraged the new Gentile followers of Jesus there (that was his name, after all!). And then decided that he needed a bit more help. So what did he do?

He went to Tarsus to look for Saul, and when he found him, he took him to Antioch. And the two of them worked together there, for a year, helping the church and teaching people about Jesus.

And it was there – in Antioch – that the followers of Jesus were first called "Christians".

Somehow Barnabas knew that this very smart Jewish man, Saul, would get along with Gentiles and be able to work well with them. That's what God had told him his job would be. However, it was not until later, when they were in Jerusalem, and met with the apostles, that Saul was at last accepted.

He wrote to his friends in Galatia:

"They saw that I had been given the task of preaching the good news to the Gentiles. This was the same as Peter did for the Jewish people. We knew that God was working through Peter — the one sent to the Jews. But God was also at work in what I was doing as one sent to the Gentiles. Everyone says that James, Peter, and John are really important leaders in the church. Well, they shook hands with Barnabas and me and recognized God's grace in us. They agreed that we should go to the Gentiles and they to the Jews."

(GALATIANS 2:7-9)

And that's what Barnabas and Saul did – their friends in Antioch sent them off on a journey, a mission, to talk to people in other cities about what God had done through Jesus. They and the other leaders of the church in Antioch were worshipping God and praying and fasting. As they did, God's Holy Spirit spoke to them. He told them to send Barnabas and Saul off on a journey, a mission, to tell people in other cities about Jesus.

So, after more praying and fasting, the leaders of the church laid their hands on Barnabas and Saul and asked God to bless their work. And off they went, with a younger helper called John Mark.

CHAPTER 5

THE SO-CALLED MAGICIAN

ACTS 13:4–20 ▢ ROMANS 2:7–11, 13–14, 17–21

When Barnabas and Saul set off on their journey, I don't think they could have imagined all the strange things they would run into. One of the strangest things happened in the first place they visited, the island of Cyprus, Barnabas' home country. In a city there, they met a Gentile and a Jew who knew each other.

The Gentile, who was in charge of the city was a good man. Saul and Barnabas might have expected that the Jew would be too, that he'd love God and do what was right, but they'd have been wrong on this occasion. Surprisingly, the Jewish man was a liar, who actually tried to keep his Gentile friend from learning about God! Oh yes, he also claimed to be a magician.

I wonder if Saul had this pair in the back of his mind when he wrote to the Romans:

"Hearing God's laws is not enough, it's those who actually obey his laws that he will call good. There are people who aren't Jews, who haven't heard God's laws. If such people were to keep God's commands, they would become the law for themselves. But you think of yourself as a Jew, and rely on the laws and think you're close to God. You know what God wants you to do through the law. You are so sure you are a guide for the blind and a light for people in the dark. You think you can be a teacher of foolish people, and those who know nothing. All because you have heard God's law which is knowledge and truth. But rather than teaching others, it is you who need to be taught!"

(ROMANS 2:13-14, 17-21)

But I said I was going to tell you about that magician...

Barnabas and Saul started their work in the town of Salamis, in eastern Cyprus. There they visited synagogues, where Jews like themselves worshipped God and prayed, and they told the people about Jesus.

Then they worked their way across the island, until they reached the town of Paphos, in the west.

The Roman proconsul, who was in charge of the whole island, lived there. His name was Sergius Paulus. Even though he was a Gentile, he knew a lot about what Jews believed and he was interested in hearing what Barnabas and Saul had to say.

The problem was that Sergius Paulus was accompanied by another man – a Jewish man who wanted to have influence over the proconsul. His name was Elymas, though he was also called Bar-Jesus. And he fancied himself a bit of a magician!

Maybe Elymas did the odd coin trick. Who knows? But he did think he could predict things. And he claimed he could hear things from God. None of which was true. The truth was that he didn't want anybody but himself to influence Sergius Paulus. And Barnabas and Saul looked like they were a threat to that.

So as they tried to tell the proconsul about Jesus, Elymas argued with them at every point and tried his best to turn Sergius Paulus against them.

But God's Holy Spirit had sent Barnabas and Saul on this journey, remember? So he gave Saul just the right words to deal with this.

"Elymas," he said. "You're a son of the devil, you are! You're fighting against all that is good, here. And with your lies and your evil intentions you are making God's straight path to this man crooked and hard.

"And so, because you are trying to blind him to God's truth, God himself will blind you, for a while, and you will not be able to see the sun!"

Now this may sound harsh, but remember, Saul himself had been blinded for a while, and that had helped him to see the truth.

Sure enough, Elymas, the so-called magician, had no power to match the power of God and reached out his arms and cried out for help, for he could no longer see.

Did this temporary blindness convince Elymas that Barnabas and Saul were telling the truth? Who knows? But it definitely convinced Sergius Paulus! He was amazed by what he saw, and believed in Jesus.

One other thing happened in Cyprus. Maybe it had to do with the name of the proconsul, Sergius Paulus. Maybe it had to do with the fact that Barnabas and Saul's mission was taking them more and more into Gentile lands. But, whatever the reason, Saul stopped going by his Jewish name, Saul, and started going by his Roman name, the name we know him by: Paul.

Paul had probably seen Gentiles accept Jesus before. But this meeting must have made it very clear to him that God now wanted to include everyone in his family, Jew and Gentile alike.

That's why he could write to the Romans:

"If you are constantly going after what is good: God's glory, honour and the things that last forever, God will give you life forever. But if you are selfish and refuse to follow truth, there is only anger and punishment in store for you. There will be trouble for everyone who works at evil, and good things for those who work at good.

> *It doesn't matter who they are, first for the Jews and then for the non-Jews. God will judge everyone the same way.*
>
> (ROMANS 2:7–11)

Oh yes, there was one more thing, from then on, the mission team would be known as Paul and Barnabas, rather than Barnabas and Paul.

CHAPTER 6

IT'S GOOD NEWS FOR EVERYONE

ACTS 13:13–52 ▣ ROMANS 3:21–25A, 28–31

Starting in Cyprus, Paul set a pattern that he never gave up on: tell the good news of Jesus to the Jews first, then to the Gentiles.

When Paul and Barnabas left the island, they sailed to a place called Perga, on the mainland. It was here that John Mark left them and went back to his home in Jerusalem, but Paul and Barnabas journeyed on to another city called Antioch. As usual, they attended the synagogue meeting and the people in charge asked Paul if there was anything he'd like to say to everyone there. Little did they know! Of course, Paul gave them an earful!

In person, he showed them the good news of Jesus through stories of the Old Testament. In his letter to the Romans, he puts the point of his message this way:

"Something new: a way to be right with God, without the law! It's been revealed now, although the Old Testament law and prophets told us about it. Being right with God is what happens to followers of Jesus when they put their trust in him, whoever they may be. Everyone has messed up and falls short of being good enough for God in his glory. But everyone can be made right through his free gift in Jesus. That was God's way of restoring things through a sacrifice he provided. We just need to trust in Jesus' sacrifice."

(ROMANS 3:21–25a)

That's the kind of message I expect Paul hit the people with when he and Barnabas arrived in a place called Antioch.

Off to Antioch. But a different Antioch, this time, a city with the same name on the way to a place called Pisidia.

When Paul and Barnabas arrived, they followed their usual practice of talking to their fellow Jews first. They went to the synagogue – the place where Jewish people prayed and learned about God.

Paul knew a lot about his Jewish faith, remember? He had been trained by the great rabbi, Gamaliel. So it makes sense that a man of his knowledge and ability was asked, by the leaders of the synagogue, to speak.

There were readings from the Jewish scriptures, the books of the Law and the Prophets. And then, as guests and visitors, Paul and Barnabas were asked to say a few encouraging words.

What did Paul do? He preached a whole sermon, that's what he did!

And Barnabas? Barnabas must have just sat there, smiling, as his partner spoke. For what Paul said proved that Barnabas had brought along just the right man for the mission.

With a wave of his hand, Paul began.

He reminded his listeners of the way that God freed their ancestors from slavery in Egypt, and then led them to a land they could call their own.

He took them, step by step, through the early history of Israel, and spoke of the judges, and Samuel the prophet, and the first king, Saul. Then he reminded them of David, Israel's greatest king – a man after God's own heart.

And that's when he began to talk about Jesus. He told his listeners that Jesus was descended from King David, and that Jesus was the saviour God had promised his people.

He told them about John the Baptist, whom God had sent to prepare his people to meet Jesus. And he made it clear that God had sent Jesus, specially, to them, the Jews, for their salvation.

Then, the tone of Paul's talk changed, as he explained how Jesus had been treated by the Jewish leaders in Jerusalem: how they had failed to recognize him as God's saviour, how they had misunderstood him, how they had convinced Pilate to put him to death, and how they had buried him in a tomb.

But Paul didn't finish there, no. Changing the tone once more, he made it clear that God's judgment was different to that of the Jewish leaders; they had condemned Jesus, but God had raised him from the dead! Many people had seen him alive. Those witnesses were actively involved in telling people about Jesus. And their own holy scripture had pointed, all along, to the fact that God would bring his special saviour back to life!

Then Paul finished his talk by telling his audience that Jesus could do for them what the law they had received from Moses could never do – set them free from their sins.

As the people left the synagogue, they pleaded with Paul and Barnabas to come again and tell them even more about Jesus.

Paul and Barnabas were more than happy to oblige. And the following week, nearly everyone in the city was there to hear what they had to say.

But some of the Jewish leaders were jealous of all the attention that Paul and Barnabas were getting. So they argued against what Paul and Barnabas said. In the end, Paul and Barnabas told them that, if that was their attitude, then they were going to tell the Gentiles about Jesus, instead.

"We spoke to you, our Jewish brothers and sisters, first," they said. "For that was the right thing to do. But if you reject what we have to say, then we will take the message of Jesus to the Gentiles. For God wants them to hear about Jesus too."

That's what they did. And when the Gentiles heard about Jesus, they believed in him, and wanted to follow him, and praised God for having been told about him.

That made the Jewish leaders even more angry, though. So they stirred up some of the city leaders against Paul and Barnabas, who then persecuted them and chased them out of the area.

But all the people who believed in Jesus – Jew and Gentile alike – lived joyfully, filled with God's Holy Spirit.

This is just what would happen time and again in Paul's life. Some Jews in a community would believe and others would get angry. Then Paul and his fellow workers would go instead to the Gentiles in that community. (But when they moved to a new town, of course, they started all over again with the Jews there.)

For Paul, it wasn't a matter of whether you believed or followed the Law that God had laid out, but whether people were willing to believe and follow God. It didn't matter whether someone belonged to Paul's own group, the Jews, or not. Again, to the Romans, he wrote:

"What we're saying is that people are made right with God by faith, not by following rules. God is not only God over the Jews. God is God over Gentiles as well! He must be the God of Gentiles too, since there is only one God. Some are obedient Jews and God will set them right with himself through their trust in him. But as for the others, who were never Jews, God will set them right with himself through their trust in him too! But do we use this trust in God to trash the law? No way."

(ROMANS 3:28-31)

Jew and Gentile, Gentile and Jew. Paul had learned that God wanted both in his family and although he was the apostle to the Gentiles, he never forgot God's love for both.

CHAPTER 7

MISTAKES IN WORSHIP

ACTS 14:1–20 ▣ ROMANS 12:1–2, 11–14, 18

Poor Paul. His own people, the Jews, didn't always understand him. But as he travelled here and there, he found that sometimes the misunderstandings of the non-Jews were even worse.

I remember Paul wrote about how we should present ourselves to God as a living sacrifices:

"Brothers and sisters, we have seen God's mercy. So here's what I think you should do: give him all of you as a living gift. This will be special and pleasing to God. It will be your spiritual act of worship. Don't keep doing things the way that everyone else does. Be changed within, make up your mind to start over again. Then you will be able to think through what God really wants — which is what is good, satisfying and perfect."

(ROMANS 12:1-2)

But once, in a little village called Lystra, people brought sacrifices to offer to Paul instead of to God! Let me tell you about it:

When Paul and Barnabas left Antioch, they went to a city called Iconium. They told the people there about Jesus, starting with the Jews, then moving on to the Gentiles.

They performed miracles, and lots of people – both Jews and Gentiles – believed what they said. Unfortunately, some of the Jewish people who did not agree with them caused trouble, and plotted to stone them. So they were forced to leave.

That's when they went to a little place called Lystra, in a district called Lycaonia.

Like lots of people in that part of the world, the Lystrans worshipped many different gods. In fact, they thought it so strange that Jews worshipped only one god that they called them "atheists", almost as if they didn't worship any god at all!

When Paul and Barnabas arrived in Lystra, they talked about Jesus, as usual. One of the men in the crowd caught Paul's attention. It was clear that he couldn't walk. And, as it turned out, he had never walked at all, for the whole of his life.

Paul looked at him. He stared at him, in fact. And then right there, in front of everyone, Paul spoke to the man and said, "Get up on your feet."

And there, right in front of everyone, that's what the man did!

He jumped up. And, more than that, he started to walk.

The crowd was amazed. And everyone began to shout, "The gods have come to visit us, in the shape of men!" This might seem like a strange thing for them to say about people they had regarded as "atheists" only a few minutes earlier. But then, seeing a man walk who'd never walked before goes a long way towards changing people's minds.

The crowd decided that Paul was their god, Hermes, because like Hermes – the messenger – he had done all the talking.

And if Paul was Hermes, they concluded that Barnabas must be the king of the gods, Zeus.

Funnily enough, Paul and Barnabas weren't aware of any of this, at first. The Lystrans were so excited by the miracle that they were talking away in their own local language, which Paul and Barnabas could not understand.

It wasn't until the priest of Zeus arrived, leading bulls to be slaughtered as a thanksgiving offering to Paul and Barnabas, that they worked out what was going on.

And then they were horrified.

They tore their clothes (what people did then to show they were horrified) and raised their voices (weirdly, what people often do when trying to make themselves

understood in another language). Then they rushed out into the crowd, shouting, "Wait! Stop! What are you doing?

"We're not gods! We're men, just like you. And the reason we're here is to turn you away from the worship of these false gods and share with you good news about the one, true God, who made heaven and earth and everything else.

"In the past, he let people of all nations find their own way, that's true. But still he gave you rain and harvests and food as evidence that he was always there, providing for you."

It was hard work. And it almost didn't work. But, in the end, Paul and Barnabas managed to talk the people out of sacrificing the bulls to them.

The problem was that it created a lot of misunderstanding, and probably the odd hurt feeling. After all, the Lystrans were only trying to do something nice – something they thought was showing their thanks for what Paul and Barnabas had done.

So when some Jews from Antioch and Iconium arrived – the Jewish people who were already unhappy with Paul and Barnabas – it didn't take much for them to turn the Lystran crowd against these men they'd mistakenly thought were gods.

The crowd picked up stones and, just as another crowd had done to Stephen, they hurled them at Paul until he stopped moving. Then they dragged his body outside the village and left him there.

The thing is that, unlike poor Stephen, Paul wasn't dead. The followers of Jesus came and gathered around him. And up he stood!

Far from being stopped by this experience, Paul worked harder still.

He and Barnabas went on to Derbe and talked about Jesus. And when they had finished there, they went back to Lystra and Iconium and Antioch, even though their enemies were still waiting for them there. They appointed elders to lead those new churches. And they encouraged them through their teaching and their brave example.

"Sometimes it's hard to follow Jesus," Paul told them. "But, that's what it takes."

Yet he had only just to begun to find out how hard it really was.

It's amazing how everyone, whether Jew or Gentile, can be eager to serve the gods that they believe in. But it can be so hard to talk and reason together about this: who really deserves worship as God? I wonder if Paul had times and places like Lystra in mind when he wrote:

"Don't let your enthusiasm die. Keep your spiritual fire, serving the Lord. Be joyful in hope, be patient in pain, be faithful in prayer. Share with God's people when they're in need. Work at being welcoming. Wish good things even to those who cause you trouble. Wish good things and not bad things... Do as much as you can to live at peace with everyone."

(ROMANS 12:11-14, 18)

Communicating clearly and living in peace – Paul tried to live that way. but it wasn't always easy, you know. Even among the followers of Jesus, there were sometimes disagreements, as we'll see shortly.

CHAPTER 8

WHAT REALLY MATTERS

ACTS 15:1–12 ▣ EPHESIANS 1:11–17

Paul loved knowing that the word of God was spreading.
He saw it spread to cities and villages, from educated
governors to simple people. They were so different from
each other yet they all came to love Jesus. Some, like
Paul himself, were Jews and had known the true God
for a long time. They knew the stories and rules of the
Old Testament. But others had been following false
gods, worshipping idols. Now they were all part of God's
family. Paul wrote about this to the Ephesians:

"We were chosen ahead of time in the plans
of the God who works everything out just
the way he wants. In that way, we who were
the first to have our hope in Christ, bring
praise to God in his glory. And now you
also are included in Christ. You heard the
word of truth and it became good news of
your rescue. Having trusted him, you were

*marked with the promised Holy Spirit. He is
a guarantee making sure we will receive what
was promised. This will be the rescue of all
of God's people, bringing praise to God in his
glory."*

(EPHESIANS 1:11–14)

*But here's the question: if we are to be one people,
shouldn't we keep to one set of rules? Now that all these
different people love God, should they all be following the
commands God had given the Jews or not? Paul and the
other people who were spreading the good news of Jesus
met together to talk about it...*

Frankly, this meeting was all about an argument.

Paul and Barnabas eventually went back to Antioch
(the Antioch in Syria, where their journey had begun).
The Christians there were keen to hear what had
happened to them on their travels. Paul and Barnabas
were even more keen to tell them. And at the heart of
their message was the good news that many Gentiles
had become followers of Jesus.

This was no small thing, especially for Paul. Before
he followed Jesus, he had obeyed the Jewish laws as
carefully and as strictly as he could. And those laws said
that good Jews were to have as little to do with Gentiles
as possible.

Yet, here he was, talking with Gentiles, spending time with Gentiles, and telling Gentiles that the long-awaited saviour that God had promised his people was meant to be a saviour to Gentiles too.

However, not every Jewish follower of Jesus saw things that way. In fact, some of those people came up from Judea to Antioch to argue with Paul and Barnabas about that very thing.

"If you want to be a follower of Jesus," they said, "you have to become a Jew first and follow all the laws and rituals and traditions that Jews follow."

"No," said Paul and Barnabas. "You don't have to become a Jew before you can become a Christian." And the argument went back and forth between the two sides.

Antioch wasn't the only place where the followers of Jesus were arguing about this, so the apostles and elders of the church in Jerusalem called a big meeting – a council – to talk through the issue and see if everyone could come to some agreement.

Paul and Barnabas were invited to attend because they had seen so many Gentiles become followers of Jesus. When they arrived in Jerusalem, they told everyone they could about what had happened on their mission – and about the Gentiles who had become Christians, in particular. But it didn't take long for the people on the other side of the argument to make their point as well.

"No, no!" they insisted. "We've said it before and we'll say it again. Jesus was a Jew. We were all Jews. So

you have to become a Jew before you can become a Christian!"

When the council began, the debate continued, each side presenting its arguments.

Finally, Peter, one of the apostles, stood up and spoke.

"You all know my story," he said. "God himself opened the door for me to tell Gentiles about Jesus. And when they heard what I said, and believed it, the Holy Spirit came on them, just like the Holy Spirit came on us on the day of Pentecost.

"I believe this was God's way of telling us that Gentiles can receive his forgiveness too, without having to obey all the Jewish laws that proved to be such a burden to us. Why should we force them to follow laws that we and all our ancestors struggled to keep? Don't you see? God wants to save both Jew and Gentile simply through the grace that Jesus showed to us all."

When Peter had finished, it was Paul and Barnabas's turn to speak. Everyone went quiet, for they knew about the amazing journey these men had taken. And so Paul and Barnabas told them how, time and time again, they had seen miracles take place and Gentile after Gentile come to believe in Jesus. In Paphos and Antioch and Iconium and Lystra, to name just a few of the places they had visited.

When they had finished, they sat down. The time had come for the council to make its decision.

I love how excited Paul gets about it – despite his Jewish upbringing, he loves the way that other people too are responding to God's gift in Jesus. As he wrote to his non-Jewish friends in Ephesus:

"That's why I've not stopped saying thank you to God for you, remembering you in all my prayers. I've been this way ever since I heard about your trust in the Lord Jesus and your love for all God's people. I keep asking that the God of Lord Jesus Christ, the glorious Father, may give you the Spirit of wisdom and knowledge of God, so that you may know him better."

(EPHESIANS 1:15-17)

However, I think Paul was secretly worried about what the meeting in Jerusalem would decide.

CHAPTER 9

A BURDEN LIFTED

ACTS 15:13–35 ▣ GALATIANS 5:16–18, 22–25

Paul believed that God gave the gift of his Spirit to help Jesus' followers. Because of sin, people often think that they want to do things that aren't good for them. We're so messed up that we might think it feels good to do what's wrong. God's Law – given to Moses – was meant to guide his people away from doing wrong. But our new guide, the Spirit, rather than steering away from wrong, steers us toward the good. I remember Paul writing about this to the Galatians:

"So, what I say is, live according to the Spirit. By doing this, you will avoid doing what your sinful self wants. The sinful self wants the bad that the Spirit doesn't and the Spirit wants the good that the sinful self doesn't. They are against each other so that you can't just do whatever you think you want. But if you let the

Spirit lead you where he wants, that's different from following a law."

(GALATIANS 5:16-18)

So Paul loved it when Peter spoke at the meeting about the Spirit coming. And he agreed with the decision that was reached.

And, now, here it comes: the council's answer! Which, strangely, had to do with strangulation. And really juicy meat.

Paul and Barnabas and everyone else at the council in Jerusalem waited anxiously to hear what the decision would be.

Would Gentiles have to become Jews and follow all the Jewish laws now that they'd become Christians? Or would they simply be allowed to follow Jesus as they were?

And would the decision keep all Christians, Jew and Gentile alike, moving forward together? Or would it split them into different groups?

Finally, James, the leader of the church in Jerusalem, stood up and delivered the verdict.

"Peter has already told us how the Spirit confirmed the acceptance of the Gentiles when God used him to reach out to them. And we know from our own scriptures, from the words of the prophet Amos, that God had always intended to show them his grace.

"So my judgment is that we should not put more of a burden on the Gentiles than is absolutely necessary. Let us write to them and say that they don't need to keep the Jewish law to be Christians. But there are a few things that they must do to show that they are no longer worshippers of pagan gods."

Now here's the thing: At their worship parties, pagan Gentiles would often drink and eat until they were sick. In some ceremonies they might even drink and bathe in blood. And they would forget all about marriage promises or other standards of behaviour. So the list of rules that the council decided they had to keep was all about that.

"Therefore, while we don't require Gentiles to take on the Jewish law," James went on, "we do require them to stop doing pagan things. They don't need to become Jews, but neither can they keep on taking part in pagan revelry.

"So they need to keep away from anything associated with the worship of idols. They need to abstain from eating the meat from any animal that has been strangled to death, or that still has the blood in it. And, finally, they need to stay away from any kind of sexual immorality."

Both sides loved this compromise. The Jewish Christians were pleased that it meant that people who used to worship false gods were moving away from everything that linked them to their previous life, while Paul and his friends were pleased that it was at last clear that no one required non-Jews to follow all the rules and regulations of Judaism.

Having made this decision, the apostles and the elders asked Paul and Barnabas to take a letter explaining all of this to the church in Antioch. And they asked two other men – Judas Barabbas and Silas – to go with them.

The letter made it clear to the Gentile Christians that the men who had told them that they had to be Jews before they could become Christians had not been sent by the church in Jerusalem. And it assured them that the guidance of God's Holy Spirit had been at the heart of the decision.

When Paul and Barnabas and Judas and Silas read out the letter to the church in Antioch, everyone was thrilled by what they heard. They were more than willing to show that their lives had been changed by God's Spirit. So they were happy to obey what was set out in the letter.

Judas and Silas stayed in Antioch for a while, encouraging the Christians there, and then went back to Jerusalem. But Paul and Barnabas remained, teaching and preaching and helping these new Christians to grow.

Paul was happy with what everyone had decided. It was in line what he had already said to the Galatians, when he wrote:

"It's as if the Spirit grew an orchard. The fruit it would produce include: love, joy, peace, patience, kindness, goodness, faithfulness, gentleness and self-control. There is no law against that! People who belong to Christ Jesus have done away with

> the sinful nature, with its wanting what's wrong. Since we live by the Spirit, let's keep in step with the Spirit."
>
> (GALATIANS 5:22-25)

And, keeping in step with the Sprit, the church did move forward in unity, reaching more and more cities.

CHAPTER 10

EVERYONE MATTERS

ACTS 16:16–24 ▣ PHILIPPIANS 2:2–8, 12, 14–15

One of the cities Paul went to after that was called Philippi. Later, he wrote a letter to the people he met there, that said:

"Here's how to make my joy complete: find a way to agree in your thinking. Share the same love, be one in spirit and of one mind. Don't do things because you think they will make you get ahead or look good. Instead put other people first. Look after each other's best interests, rather than your own."

(PHILIPPIANS 2:2-4)

And this was precisely the attitude that Paul modelled when he was there in Philippi. Why, I remember this

71

small business he ran across. They were fortune-tellers...

When God told Paul and his new co-worker, Silas, to go to Macedonia to tell the people who lived there about Jesus, that's exactly what they did.

They crossed the sea and eventually made their way to the capital city of Macedonia – a place called Philippi.

Outside the city gates, down by the river, they found a place where people met to pray. There, they met a business woman called Lydia, who specialized in selling expensive purple cloth. When they told her about Jesus, she and everyone in her household were baptized. Paul and Silas were off to a great start!

The next day, as they made their way back to that place of prayer, things looked even better. They met a girl who cried out, in a voice everyone could hear, "These men serve The Most High God. They have come here to show you the way to salvation!"

"Brilliant!" thought Paul. "That's bound to help."

The girl met them the next day too. And shouted exactly the same thing. And it happened the day after that, as well. It kept happening, in fact, for many days. The same girl. The very same words. But nothing more.

Eventually, Paul decided that something wasn't quite right with that girl. And when he looked into it, he discovered the truth.

The girl was a slave girl, who made lots of money for her masters by telling fortunes. And how did she do that? There was a demon inside her, that's how.

It all made sense, now. Paul remembered the stories he had heard about Jesus – how people with demons inside would call out after him, as well, saying true things about him, just like the girl was doing.

Her words might have helped Paul, might have drawn attention to what he and Silas were trying to do. But none of that mattered, if the girl was in the grip of a demon.

So the next time the girl met them, and the next time she cried out, "These men serve The Most High God. They have come here to show you the way to salvation!" Paul's reaction was completely different.

Angry at the power the demon held over her, and angry that her human masters were using that power to make money, Paul addressed the demon and said, "In the name of Jesus Christ, I command you to come out of this girl!"

And that's what the demon did. It flew right out of her, like something flying out a window. At last, the girl was free!

The problem was that her masters saw their profits flying out the window as well. And they were not very happy. Not happy, at all. So they grabbed hold of Paul and Silas and dragged them to the marketplace, in the middle of the city, where the magistrates passed judgment.

"These men are Jews and they are causing trouble in our city!" The girl's masters shouted. "We're all good Roman citizens – and these men are telling us to do

thing we know are against our laws!"

None of that was true. The girl's masters were simply trying to get people on their side, and they thought that pointing out that Paul and Silas were foreigners with foreign ideas would do the trick. And it did!

So the crowd sided against Paul and Silas, and attacked them. And the magistrates sided against them too, and ordered them to be beaten.

And when Paul and Silas had been stripped of their clothes and beaten with rods till they bled, they were hauled off to jail, where their feet were bound fast in stocks.

It had all started out so well, this trip to Philippi. But now they were in pain, and in jail, all because they had put the needs of a slave girl before their own, and asked God to rescue her.

The question now was, "Who would rescue them?"

See what I mean about Paul? Even when people were willing to think he was a big deal, he didn't care – he was more interested in helping that girl than in what people thought of him. I think he learned that from Jesus' teachings and example. In that letter I mentioned, he wrote to the slave girl and other people back in Philippi:

"When it comes to how you are with others, think of it the way that Jesus did. Even though he was divine, he didn't think of his equality with God as something he should insist on in order to benefit himself. Instead, he made himself nothing... he humbled himself by becoming someone who could die. He was willing even to suffer death on the cross! ... So, my dear friends, as you have always obeyed... do everything without grumbling or arguing. In that way you may become blameless and pure. You'll be 'children of God without fault in a warped and crooked time'. Then you will shine among them like stars in the sky."

(PHILIPPIANS 2:5-8, 12, 14-15)

I love to think of that young girl Paul helped in Philippi. Once she was only a celebrity, but now she's a star! Paul, on the other hand, often got into trouble by doing good, as we'll see.

CHAPTER 11

HAPPY IN JAIL!

ACTS 16:25–40 ▣ PHILIPPIANS 1:7–9, 12–13; 4:4–9

Yes, Paul spent a fair amount of time in jail. That time in Philippi wasn't the first and it wouldn't be the last. His friends in the city knew it really meant something when he wrote in his letter to them:

"Be glad in the Lord all the time. Let me repeat that: Be glad! Let your gentleness be clear to everyone. The Lord is coming soon. Don't be worried about anything. Whatever happens, prayerfully and thankfully ask God for what you need. And God's peace, which is beyond what we can understand, will guard your hearts and your minds in Christ Jesus. Finally, brothers and sisters, focus on things that are excellent or worthy of praise — whatever is true or noble or right or pure or lovely or admirable. Do the things that you have learned and

*heard from me or seen me do. And the God
of peace will be with you."*

(PHILIPPIANS 4:4-9)

*Well, Paul was doing all those things when he was in the
Philippian jail....*

It was late. It was dark. The dim light from a torch cast
striped shadows across the floor of the prison cell.

Paul groaned. His friend Silas groaned too. For there
were stripes across their backs as well – the result of a
beating ordered by the magistrate. Their "reward" for
healing a girl possessed by a demon.

With their feet bound in stocks, all they could
do was shift and squirm and try their best to find a
comfortable position. Or, to be fair, a position that was
less uncomfortable.

But there was one more thing they could do. They
could pray.

God had brought them across the sea to Philippi.
There was no question about that. And God's power
had set the slave girl free from the demon's hold. There
was no question there, either. So God was surely in that
prison with them. And all they needed to do was speak
to him, and worship him, and trust their lives to him.

And that's why their prayers turned to songs. And
that's why, backs bleeding and feet shackled, they could

praise God, even in a prison cell.

And that's also why their impromptu worship time was interrupted by a deep and angry growl.

"Shut up, you!" shouted the jailer, a big burly bear of a man. "We'll have none of your foreign gabbling about foreign gods! That's what put you here, in the first place."

Then he shook his fist, and rattled his sword along the bars for good measure. "Now go to sleep!"

The two men fell silent, but only until they could hear the jailer's rumbling snore, echoing from outside the prison door. Then the prayers resumed, and the songs, too, for well over an hour, right up to midnight, when the worship was interrupted once again.

It was just a tremor, at first. A fizz in the air. A silent shimmer. A gentle shake. And so caught up were they in their worship, that Paul and Silas hardly noticed. But when the earthquake struck with full force, there was no missing its effect.

Floors cracked. And dust rose. And men screamed, out of panic, first, and then for joy, as their chains fell off and the prison doors burst open.

The jailer woke with a start. He stumbled about. He peered through the dust. And when he saw the open doors, he fell, shaking, to his knees.

His prisoners were long gone, surely. And no matter what the circumstances, they were his responsibility. So this was his failure.

What would he tell his wife? And, more than that, what would he tell his masters? Like any jailer, he knew that death would be his punishment. Better to do it now, quickly, by my own hand, thought the jailer, than to wait for someone else to do it. Someone less merciful. Someone less... efficient.

So, solemnly, he drew his sword. But before the jailer could bury the sword into his body, a voice rang out: "Wait! Don't hurt yourself! We're all still here."

The jailer recognized that voice. It belonged to the foreigner who had just been arrested. So he grabbed a torch and rushed through the cells. Everyone was, indeed, still there. And so, trembling, that big bear of a man fell to his knees again, before Paul and Silas, and asked a simple question, "What do I have to do to be saved?"

The jailer was just looking for a solution to his troubles, but Paul saw it as an opportunity to change the man's life forever. So he told him all about Jesus. And about how Jesus had come to save everyone from death. Everyone imprisoned by sin.

Once the other prisoners were safely locked up again, the jailer took Paul and Silas to his house. He dressed their wounds and fed them. And the more they talked, the more he and his family understood. This wasn't some foreign nonsense they were speaking. It was the truth.

So they were all baptized – the jailer and his family. And when he came up from the water, he gave Paul and Silas a big wet bear hug.

Then they all prayed. And sang songs. Just like when they were in prison. Because, prisoner and jailer alike, they were all out of prison now.

What a mixed bunch Paul met in Philippi, business women, slaves, and jailers. And he loved them all. Maybe they worried about him, especially the jailer, when they heard later that he had been put into jail again. But he wrote in his letter to them:

"I hold you in my heart. And whether I'm locked up in chains or out talking about the good news and showing its truth, all of you share in God's grace with me. God knows that I'm always thinking of you. I care about you like Christ Jesus does. And this is my prayer: that your love would keep growing more and more in knowledge and wisdom...

I want you to know, brothers and sisters, that the things that have happened to me will actually help the good news to spread. In fact, it has now been made clear to the whole Palace Guard and everyone else that Christ is the reason I'm locked up here."

(PHILIPPIANS 1:7-9, 12-13)

And you know, I'll bet after reading that, the jailer remembered the time when Paul was in his jail and chuckled, saying, "Those palace guards have no idea yet who they're dealing with!"

CHAPTER 12

SERVING A DIFFERENT KING

ACTS 17:1–14 ▪ 1 THESSALONIANS 1:6–9; 2:13

Shortly after Philippi, Paul and Silas visited the city of Thessalonika, where the Jewish meeting house was used by both Jews and non-Jews. Quite a few of them were happy to hear the good news of Jesus that Paul brought. Writing to them later, Paul recalled this about the reception he received:

"You began to act just like us and like the Lord. You suffered a lot but you welcomed the message with the joy that the Holy Spirit brings. And so you became an example to other followers from Macedonia and Greece. The Lord's message rang out from you not only to those places, but your trust in God has become known everywhere so we don't even need to say anything about you.

> *Instead other people tell us of the way you*
> *accepted us. And they tell about how you*
> *turned from false gods to serve the true*
> *and living God."*
>
> (1 THESSALONIANS 1:6-9)

But, as ever, it didn't go completely without a hitch. In fact, there was a riot!

That's right. A riot!

When Paul and Silas arrived in Thessalonika they went, as usual, to the synagogue on the Jewish holy day. For three weeks in a row, Paul went and taught the people there about Jesus.

He not only spoke to the Jews, but also to Gentiles who were interested in what Jews believed - people whom the Jews called God-fearers.

He showed them, from the scriptures, that God had promised to send a rescuer, the Messiah, to his people, and he was actually supposed to die and rise again. Then he made the case that Jesus of Nazareth had fulfilled all those promises.

And, guess what?

Some of the Jews believed what Paul had to say. Which was great. And there was also a huge response from the God-fearers! Many of them decided to follow Jesus, as well as some women who were important leaders in Thessalonika.

Now this was good news for Paul and Silas, but not such good news for the rest of the Jews in the synagogue. They were jealous of Paul and Silas's success, particularly among the God-fearers, so they decided to make trouble for them.

They kicked off a riot with some of the most violent and wicked men in the city. Then they led them, fists and voices raised, to the house of a man named Jason, where Paul and Silas were staying. They weren't in, though, so they grabbed poor Jason and some other Christians who

happened to be there, and dragged them before the city authorities.

"There are certain men who have turned the world upside-down," they cried. "And they have come, here, to our city! They say that there is another king besides Caesar. A king they call Jesus. And Jason has given them a place to stay."

It didn't matter whether the mob had misunderstood Paul and Silas, or whether they were just putting the worst possible spin on what they taught. The fact is that the city authorities were worried when they heard this. The last thing they wanted in their town was a group of revolutionaries who wanted to replace the Roman emperor with a different king.

So they ordered Jason and the others to pay them bond money before they would set them free. If things calmed down, they would get the money back. If they didn't, the authorities would keep the money - and there would be more trouble besides!

That night, the Christians in Thessalonika sneaked Paul and Silas out of the city, and sent them on their way, to a place called Berea.

There was a synagogue in Berea too. So, just as before, Paul did not hesitate to make his presence known there, and to teach the people exactly the same things he had taught the Jews and God-fearers in Thessalonika.

The response of the Jews in Berea, however, was very different from that of the people in Thessalonika. They weren't jealous, and they weren't afraid. No, they were genuinely curious about Paul's teaching. They were keen to learn more. And they searched their scriptures diligently, to make sure that what Paul taught them was right.

And the result?

Many of the Jews followed Jesus, as well as many God-fearing Gentile men and women.

All would have ended well, if the Jews in Thessalonika had not heard what was happening. But they did, and they brought their rioting mob to Berea, to stir up trouble.

The Christians didn't waste any time. They put Paul on a boat, while Silas and their young helper, Timothy, stayed behind to support the new Christians there. At first, it looked as if they might have the harder job. But, Paul was bound for Athens, where he would face one of the biggest challenges of his missionary career.

I often wonder whether the accusers were right. Paul did teach about another king with an even higher authority than Caesar. But then again, Jesus is an entirely different kind of king. Not a human leader, but God's leader. As Paul wrote to them later:

"And we thank God all the time. When you heard the good news from us, you didn't accept it as people talking. Instead, you took it for what it really is: God talking. And his message changed you believers!"

(1 THESSALONIANS 2:13)

Looking back now, it's easy to see that Paul and his friends did turn the world upside down through their message. But, as we'll find out, Paul didn't always feel very successful.

CHAPTER 13

"AN UNKNOWN GOD"

ACTS 17:25-34 ▣ ROMANS 1:20–25, 28–29A, 31–32

If you'd asked Paul "where did the human race go wrong?", he'd say, "before we went anywhere!" It's a little like a treasure map that tells you to "Start at the big oak, take nine paces north, and so on". But if someone doesn't know their trees, and starts at the palm tree rather than at the oak tree, then even if they follow the directions perfectly, they'll end up at the wrong place.

Not recognizing that God is the starting point of everything is making that kind of mistake.

Paul described this when he wrote to people in the city of Rome:

"Really, people have no excuse. They knew there must be a God, but they refused to give him glory or thank him. They thought of ways around what was true and it was as if all the lights went out in their hearts and minds. They claimed to be so very smart, but *instead became fools. They traded the glory of God who lives forever for images made to look like people or birds or animals or reptiles... They had exchanged the truth of God for a lie. And all the things they should have given to the God who created them, they gave instead to created things."*

(ROMANS 1:20-25)

Maybe you know what he's talking about?

Idols. Statues of false gods. Statues that people worshipped instead of worshipping the one true God.

That's what Paul saw as he walked around Athens, waiting for Silas and Timothy to join him. The idols were everywhere, hundreds and hundreds of them. And Paul was disturbed by every idol he saw.

He had been raised a good Jew. So, from his childhood, he had been taught one thing, above all: there was only one God. And he, and he alone, deserved to be worshipped. "Worship the Lord your God, and him only shall you serve." It was the first of the commandments that Moses had brought down from the mountain. And the second? "You shall make no carved images, no idols."

It was clear to Paul that if there was any place that needed rescuing from the worship of idols, any place that needed to hear about the one true God and Jesus his Messiah, it was Athens.

So Paul went to the synagogue, as was his custom, and spoke to the Jews first. And he also went into the marketplace, and told anyone who would listen all about Jesus and how he had come back from the dead. Come back to live forever.

Now, Athens was filled with teachers and philosophers who loved to talk about new ideas and beliefs. And when they heard Paul, they were intrigued.

"What's he babbling about?" someone asked.

"Some strange new foreign god," someone else replied.

So they invited Paul to speak to the Areopagus, a gathering of the leading men of Athens.

"The things you teach sound strange to us," they said. "Tell us more, please, about what you believe."

And so Paul did.

"Men of Athens," he said. "As I walked around your city, I could tell that you were very religious. I passed idol after idol, dedicated to every kind of deity. In fact, I even came across an altar to an 'Unknown God'.

"Well, it's that 'Unknown God' that I want to make known to you, today.

"He is the God who made this world, and everything in it. He is the Lord of heaven and earth.

"He doesn't live in man-made temples. He is not made by human hands. No, it is by his hands that we are made. Every human in every place. Every nation and every race. Made to seek him, to feel our way towards him, and to find him.

"Why, even your own poets have hinted at this truth:

"'In him we live and move and have our being,' says one.

"'We are his children,' says another.

"So if we are God's children, how could he possibly be a mere statue, made of gold or silver or stone? An image, crafted by man's hands, sprung from man's imagination?

"No, that is ignorance, pure and simple. And, until now, God has overlooked that ignorance. But now the time has come for everyone, everywhere to turn their backs on that view of God and to live a different way. For he has set a day of judgment for this world, and approved one righteous man as judge, by raising him from the dead."

The men of Athens had listened intently to this point. But when Paul started talking about a man coming back from the dead, some of them made fun of him.

Others, still intrigued, told him they would like to hear more.

And a few, including Dionysius, the Areopagite, and a woman named Damaris, left with him and followed Jesus.

And left their man-made idols behind.

Just as in Thessalonika, Paul didn't always find it easy to get people to think again about God or about Jesus. He wrote about this to the people in Rome:

"Some people give up on God. They fall into a habits of thinking that are wrong and ways of acting that they shouldn't. Such people become filled with evil and greed... they get to the point where they cannot change their way of thinking, cannot believe, cannot feel for themselves or for others. They know that God said that continuing to do what's wrong will lead to death. Even if they believe that, they nevertheless continue to do what's wrong and approve of others who are the same."

(ROMANS 1:28-29a; 31-32)

Paul knew that everyone messes things up again and again. Paul also knew that Jesus came to break this cycle. And that's why Paul spread the good news of Jesus.

CHAPTER 14

LOVE AND REJECTION

ACTS 18:1–18 ▣ 1 CORINTHIANS 13:1–7

It all sounds wonderful sometimes. Paul got to travel all over the world, and people would gather in large crowds to hear him speak. And those who came to follow Jesus looked up to him and regarded him as special. But most of it wasn't really like that. Travelling was such hard, tiring work. And although he knew he was speaking the truth about what Jesus had done, Paul felt sadness and disappointment when his own people, the Jews, and others rejected his message or caused trouble. There were some really sad times. It was Paul's relationship with Jesus and his love for the people that kept him going.

He wrote to the Christians in Corinth:

"You know, if I could speak in different languages, of humans and of angels, if I didn't have love, I would only be like a noisy bell or clanging cymbal. And say I was gifted in seeing the future and could understand

> secret things and all knowledge — and if
> I had belief so great that I could use it
> to move a mountain. If I had all that, but
> didn't have love, I'd be nothing. Say I gave
> everything I had to poor people, even gave
> up my own body to be burned. If it's without
> love, I would gain nothing."
>
> (1 CORINTHIANS 13:1-3)

The city of Corinth was one those places he found especially hard.

It was to this city that Paul went when he left Athens.

Things went pretty well there, at first.

He met two Jewish followers of Jesus, just like him. Their names were Aquila and Priscilla, and they had just arrived in Corinth, because Emperor Claudius, had recently ordered every Jew living in Rome to leave the city.

But being Jewish wasn't the only thing Paul had in common with Aquila and Priscilla. Like him, they had been trained as tent makers when they were young. So they all made tents together, always looking for every opportunity to tell the people of Corinth about Jesus.

As usual, Paul went to the synagogue first, to explain to his own people how Jesus was their long-awaited Messiah. But most of the Jews simply didn't accept what Paul told them. And, worse than that, they called Paul all sorts of ugly names and said horrible things about him.

It was really discouraging, because Paul was desperate for his own people to understand and accept the amazing thing that God had done for them, through Jesus. But, in the end, Paul decided he simply had to move on.

"You've made your own bed," he said. "And now you can sleep in it. I've tried my hardest. The fault is yours, not mine. From now on, I'm going to focus on the Gentiles in Corinth."

And that's what he did.

He worked from the house of a man named Titius Justus, who was one of those God-fearers – a Gentile interested in what Jews believed.

The thing is, though, Titius Justus's house was right next door to the synagogue! And that can't have made the Jews who opposed Paul very happy at all. What's more, they must have been really angry when Crispus, the leader of the synagogue, decided to follow Jesus, along with everyone else in his house.

Paul carried on, and many, many more Corinthians believed in Jesus and were baptized. It was still hard, though. And the opposition of the Jews continued to discourage him.

God understood that, so, one night, he came to Paul in a vision.

"Don't be afraid, Paul," the Lord said. "And don't be silent, either. Keep on talking about me. Nobody will hurt you, I promise, for I have many followers in this city."

Paul stayed in Corinth for a year and a half. But then, when a man named Gallio was the Roman official in charge of the area, the Jews got together and dragged Paul before him.

They accused Paul of breaking the law with the things he taught. But Gallio would have none of it.

"If this man had committed a violent crime," he told them, "or broken the law in some other way, then you would have every right to bring him before me. But your complaint is about words and names and things that have to do with your religion. So it's not my place to judge."

And with that, he sent them away.

So, true to God's promise, Paul was not harmed in Corinth. And, faithful to God, Paul carried on spreading the good news of Jesus throughout the city.

Even though many Corinthians became Christians, Paul often found them difficult to be with. Sometimes they would cause each other pain. But they stretched Paul in his practice of love. He wrote to them:

"Love is patient, love is kind. Love doesn't get jealous. Love doesn't brag, it's not proud of itself. Love isn't rude, it doesn't try to get its own way all the time. Love doesn't easily get angry and it doesn't keep score. Love is unhappy with what's bad, but rejoices about truth. Love can bear anything. Love always trusts, always hopes, it just keeps on going."

(1 CORINTHIANS 13:4–7)

Despite all the difficult relationships that he had with people in Corinth, Paul kept on going.

CHAPTER 15

BROKEN RULES AND BROKEN IMAGES

ACTS 19:21–41 ▣ EPHESIANS 1:19–21; 2:8–10

Paul was used to dealing with trouble from his own Jewish people and their jealousy, and also from those who believed in many different gods. He must have felt as if he was walking a tightrope: he followed the rules of the authorities as best he could, while at the same time being very aware of having a Lord who was above all earthly leaders and rulers. This especially struck Paul in Ephesus and he wrote to the people there:

"God's great power really can't be compared with anything else. And it works for us who trust in him. That power is like the authority he showed in raising Jesus Christ from the dead. And now he's seated with God, right by his side, in heaven. So he is far, far above all rulers and authorities,

> *far above all powers and governments. He is*
> *far above any title like president or prime*
> *minister or king. And not just for now, but*
> *forever."*
>
> (EPHESIANS 1:19–21)

Paul worked for a higher authority, but that didn't stop him from getting into hot water with local authorities and their "gods".

Paul was in the city of Ephesus, a city famous for the worship of the Greek goddess Artemis. The Greeks believed that she was the daughter of Zeus, king of the gods, and sister to Apollo. She was goddess of hunting and wild animals and childbirth. And Ephesus was the site of the temple dedicated to her.

As you probably remember from Paul's visit to Athens, he didn't have much time for any god but the one true God, the maker of everything. Idols were statues of false gods, as far as he was concerned. It was wrong to worship them. And he didn't mind saying so.

This put him in conflict with one particular citizen of Ephesus: Demetrius the silversmith.

Demetrius and his workmen made little silver statues of Artemis, which they sold to the people who came to visit her temple. So, from his point of view, Paul's preaching about the uselessness of idols was bad for business.

He called together all the other craftsmen in Ephesus who were involved in the idol-making trade – men who worked in wood and stone and metal – and delivered an impassioned speech.

"Men," he said, "we are all in the same business. We all know where our wealth comes from – the making and selling of idols. We make any god. Any, any, any god. That has always been our slogan, and the source of our income.

"But then this troublemaker Paul comes along, preaching his nonsense that gods made by human hands are not gods at all. And people believe him! Not only across the whole of Asia Minor, but more worryingly, here in Ephesus, as well.

"If we are not careful, this man is going to put us out of business." And, in case it sounded as if he was only concerned about money, Demetrius added, "And it could also threaten the temple and the standing of the great goddess Artemis, who is worshipped all over the world."

Their income (and their goddess) threatened, the craftsmen started a riot. Shouting "Great is Artemis of the Ephesians!", they grabbed two of Paul's co-workers, Gaius and Aristarchus, and dragged them, followed by a great crowd, to the great amphitheatre in Ephesus.

Paul wanted to join his friends, but the other Christians in Ephesus talked him out of it. It was just too dangerous.

Meanwhile, the crowd was going crazy. Some people were shouting one thing. Some, another. And most people didn't even know why they were there. It was mayhem!

The Jews in the crowd convinced one of their own, a man called Alexander, to stand up and try to explain the problem that Jews had with idols. But as soon as the craftsmen heard that he was Jewish, they shouted out, even more loudly, "Great is Artemis of the Ephesians!"

Finally, the town clerk managed to quiet the crowd.

"Men of Ephesus," he said. "Everybody knows how important our city is. Does not the temple of the great goddess Artemis stand here in our midst?

"Yes, the greatness of our city is clear to everyone. So you have nothing to worry about. And certainly nothing to riot about. Calm down!

"As for the men you dragged in here, they haven't, personally, said anything against our goddess. So, Demetrius and the rest of you craftsmen, if you do have a problem with these men, the courts are open. Take your complaints to the judges, where they belong. This is not the place!

"The last thing this city needs is a riot. And you're going to be charged with starting one for no reason at all, if you don't settle down."

He must have been a very persuasive speaker, that town clerk. For when he had finished, the crowd dispersed. And everyone went back to their business.

Those souvenir sellers in Ephesus were really worried about their handiwork. But Paul knew that God was more worried about his handiwork: people who need Jesus because they can't get to God by anything they can do. Later he wrote to his friends there:

"For it is God's gift to you that he saved you through your trust in him. You can't do it by yourselves. The good things we do can't save us, so no one can brag about themselves. Instead, we are God's workmanship — he made us. And he made us to do good things, and prepared those things for us to do ahead of time."

(EPHESIANS 2:8-10)

Paul made sure his friends in Ephesus were taken care of, even when he was prevented from returning to the city in person. I'll tell you about that next.

CHAPTER 16

A SAD FAREWELL

ACTS 20:13–38 ▣ EPHESIANS 3:7–9, 12–13

Paul was full of surprises. For instance, he started out as someone who worked against Jesus and his followers, but then became someone who would do anything for him. Here's another surprising thing: most people think of him as someone who travelled to town after town, telling the good news and then moving on. And that's true enough. But there's more to it than that, because he rarely forgot about those he had met. He cared for the people who came to trust in God, keeping in touch through letters and going back to visit them when he could. Paul didn't see himself just as a pioneer and leader, creating churches. He saw himself as a tour guide and servant of Jesus and of the people of God. He wrote:

"It was because of God's gift, delivered to me with power, that I became a servant of this good news. I'm probably the least worthy of all of God's people and yet he gave

> me this gift: I get to share with non-Jews
> the endless mountain of treasure that is
> Christ. The God who created the universe
> has kept these things secret for centuries,
> and me? I get to be everyone's tour guide to
> them!"
>
> (EPHESIANS 3:7-9)

Paul couldn't go back to Ephesus, he was in too much trouble with the authorities. But he could still write to them – the words above are from a letter to them. He also met with leaders from the Ephesian church again, although they had to do it in another town.

Paul was on his way to Jerusalem again. God's Holy Spirit had told him to go there. He wanted to arrive in time for the Feast of Pentecost. But there was one thing he needed to do first: speak to leaders of the church in Ephesus.

He hadn't just started that church and then moved on. No, Paul worked with the new Christians there for three years, through good times and bad, teaching and encouraging and supporting them. He had friends in Ephesus, friends he was going to miss. Sadly, however, it was too dangerous for Paul to return.

So when the ship he was sailing in docked at Miletus, a town not far from Ephesus, Paul arranged for the leaders of the church to come and meet him there.

This is what he told them:

"You all know my story. Of course you do.

"I was there, with you, from the moment I set foot in Asia Minor. I worked humbly with you, but it wasn't always easy. There were tears. There were struggles. Particularly when the Jews plotted against me.

"But despite all that, I did not shy away from doing what I thought was best for you. Teaching you, out in the open and from house to house. And making it clear to both Jews and Greeks the need to turn away from what displeases God and turn instead, in faith, towards the Lord Jesus.

"And now, the Holy Spirit tells me that I need to travel to Jerusalem. He doesn't say exactly what will happen to me there, apart from the fact that I will face pain and prison, wherever I go.

"I'm not bothered about that. My own life is worth nothing. What does concern me though, is that I might not have the chance to finish the job that the Lord Jesus gave me – to tell as many people as possible about the good news of God's grace.

"Sadly, none of you standing here, who heard that good news from my lips, will ever see my face again. I have no regrets, though, for I told you everything I know about God. So here's what I want you to do.

"Dedicate yourselves to caring for the 'flock' God gave you to shepherd. As elders, as overseers, watch over the church – the church Jesus saved with his own blood.

"For when I am gone, dangerous 'wolves' will try to tear your church apart, both from without and from within. They will try to teach you things that are wrong and drag you away from what is true.

"So be alert. Watch out for them. And remember that I was here, for three years, making sure that everyone knew what was right, even when it brought me to tears.

"And so I leave you in God's hands, and in the truth that comes from his word – truth that will build you up and prepare you for the inheritance God has for you.

"Oh, and one more thing. I want to make it absolutely clear that I did none of this for silver or gold. I worked with my own hands, remember, to provide for myself and for those who worked with me. And I did it to set you an example of how we are to care for the poor. Never forget what the Lord Jesus said: 'It is more blessed to give than to receive.'"

When Paul had finished speaking, he dropped to his knees and prayed for the elders. They all wept together, and the elders hugged Paul and kissed him because they knew that they would never see him again.

Then they escorted him to the ship. And, as he sailed away, they waved their sad goodbyes.

God is loving and powerful. But Paul knew well that life as a follower of God would not always be easy either for him or for people like the Ephesian believers. Or for us! He wrote later to the people in Ephesus:

"Because of Jesus, we can come to God with freedom and confidence. I'm asking you, then, not to be discouraged because of anything bad that happens to me because of you — it's all for your good."

(EPHESIANS 3:12–13)

This is the secret of Paul's ability to keep going: even in the hard times he had a sense of how fortunate he was to be involved in showing people the beauty of God's mysteries and a sense that God would bring good out of every situation.

CHAPTER 17

BEING JEWISH IN JERUSALEM

ACTS 21:17–36 ◫ ROMANS 2:28 – 3:4A, 9–11

Just like Jesus, Paul never really valued what could be seen on the outside as much as what was true on the inside. I remember Paul once wrote to the Romans:

"A person is not a Jew because you see them acting like one. By looking at a person, you can't really tell whether they follow God or not. No, a person is a Jew if they keep God's word inside, if there are marks, they are marks on the heart. And these are marks made by the Spirit, not by the written law. People make a big deal of things that can be seen, but God praises what is in the heart.

"Is there anything good about being a Jew with all the outward signs of that? Yes, lots!

> And the greatest is this — they have been
> entrusted with God's own words. OK, so some
> didn't respond to God's news with faith. But
> there's no way that their lack of faith will stop
> God from seeing things through."
>
> (ROMANS 2:28 - 3:4a)

The crazy thing is that when Paul was arrested in Jerusalem, he was among his own people, the Jews, and doing something they approved of! Yet again...

Yeah, you've guessed it. More trouble!

When Paul finally arrived in Jerusalem, he went to see James, the leader of the church there, and all the elders.

He told them about all the cities he had visited. He told them about all the Gentiles who had decided to follow Jesus. And when they heard what Paul had to say, they thanked God for all that he had done.

"There's just one problem," James explained. "Thousands of the Jewish followers of Jesus, here in Jerusalem, are still keen to obey all of the Jewish laws and rituals and traditions. I can't tell you how important this is to them."

Paul nodded. He understood. He'd been there.

"The thing is," James went on, "there have been rumours that you've told Jewish Christians that there was no need for them to obey the laws that came from

Moses. And that has made the Jewish Christians here in Jerusalem very angry."

Paul shook his head. "No. Never," he said.

"We know your background," James assured him. "So we know these rumours are not true. But as you are here in Jerusalem, we need to find some way for you to assure the Jewish followers of Jesus that you still have the deepest respect for the Jewish law."

"Agreed," nodded Paul.

"So here's what we want you to do," said James. "Four of these Jewish Christians will be going to the Temple, over the next seven days, to be purified by a Jewish ritual – a ritual well known to you. We want you to join them, to be purified with them, and to pay whatever costs are involved for the five of you.

"We think this will convince the Jewish Christians that you, too, are dedicated to the Law of Moses, and that the rumours they have heard are simply not true."

Paul nodded again. This made sense.

"Finally, and to be perfectly clear, we are not saying that Gentiles have to obey the Law of Moses," James concluded. "We sent them that letter, remember, saying that all they had to do was stay away from anything that smacked of pagan worship – meat offered to idols, meat that had been strangled, blood, and sexual immorality."

Paul did remember. He'd been there, hadn't he? And he also understood the wisdom of being sensitive to the Jewish followers of Jesus. So he did what James and the elders told him to do and joined the four men, in the Temple.

And that's when the trouble started.

The Jewish Christians were very happy with what Paul was doing. But in the Temple, there were of course lots of Jews who continued with their old ways and had not become followers of Jesus. And some of them just happened to be the very same people who had opposed Paul during his mission trips.

When they recognized him, they grabbed hold of Paul and shouted, "Help us, Men of Israel! Help! He's here. In the Temple. The man who has been telling everyone, everywhere, lies about our laws, and our people, and this very place. Why, he has even sneaked a Gentile in here, among us."

None of this was true. And as for the Gentile? Yes, Paul had been with a Gentile called Trophimus before he entered the Temple, but he hadn't sneaked him in. Not at all.

None of that mattered, though. The crowd in the Temple believed Paul's enemies, and they dragged him out of the Temple and beat him. They would have killed him, had their cries and angry words, not been silenced by another sound: the clatter of spears and shields and swords, and the regular beat of soldier's feet on the hard ground.

The Roman tribune, in charge of keeping the peace, had been informed of the riot. So he brought soldiers and officers to calm the crowd.

"Arrest this man!" he ordered, pointing at Paul. And the soldiers seized Paul and bound him with a pair of chains.

"Now, then!" the tribune said. "Somebody tell me what this man has done."

And that's when the shouting started up again.

Some shouted one thing. Some another. It was chaos, and the tribune couldn't work out what was going on.

"Take him back to the barracks!" the tribune ordered his soldiers. "And we will sort this out, in our own time."

So the soldiers did. In fact, they had to carry Paul because the crowd was so anxious to get their hands on him and kill him.

"Away with him!" they shouted. "Away with him!"

So Paul, who had simply been trying to do the right thing, finished the day in chains, in a Roman barracks.

But at least he was safe. And alive. For without the tribune's intervention, the crowd would surely have killed with him.

Poor old Paul, nowhere was really safe for him. In foreign cities like Athens and Ephesus, he got in trouble for attacking their gods, and even here, worshipping the same God as his own people and following the old customs, he didn't fare much better. It was hard for him to admit, but even his own people weren't following their God. He wrote about it to the Romans:

"So what can we be sure of? Are we Jews better than non-Jews? Not really. We've already said that Jews and non-Jews alike are all likely to do wrong and mess things up. This is even written in the Jewish scriptures, the Old Testament: 'There is no one who does right all the time, not even one. And there is not one who understands and looks to God.'"

(ROMANS 3:9–11. SEE PSALM 14:1–2)

The last time Paul met with a High Priest, it had been when he was Saul, the enemy of Christians, asking for a letter of recommendation. What a different situation he was in now!

CHAPTER 18

DISPUTES
IN JERUSALEM

ACTS 22:30 – 23:11 ▪ 1 CORINTHIANS 15:21–26, 55, 57–58

Paul had become a follower of Jesus because Jesus
appeared to him. And that was after Jesus had died.
Which meant that Jesus was still doing things after he
was dead! Death was not the end. And Paul believed
Jesus was coming back for him – for all of us – defeating
death forever. Paul really looked forward to that! He
wrote as much to the Corinthians:

"Death came about because of one person,
but now the defeat of death also comes
because of a person. So, because of Adam all
of us die, but in Christ, all will be made alive
for ever. Each in order: Christ is the first.
And then, when he returns, those who belong
to him will be raised. That's when the end
will come for every dominion, authority, and

123

> *power, and Jesus will hand everything over to*
> *God the Father. Jesus is in charge and will*
> *be until he's on top of every enemy. And the*
> *last enemy he'll take care of is death."*

(1 CORINTHIANS 15:21-26)

Paul grew up as a Pharisee, and that meant that he was taught that life continued after death. Another group of Jews, the Sadducees, thought death was the end. And Jerusalem was the one city in the whole empire where the Sadducees were in charge. So I remember once, when Paul appeared before the leaders of both parties, he really made use of this difference.

The tribune didn't know what to do with Paul. He couldn't work out why the crowd hated him. So, sadly, he decided to beat the truth out of him.

"Stretch him out and whip him," he ordered one of his officers.

Following the tribune's orders, the officer tied up Paul in a way that made sure that the whipping would really hurt. But before even one blow was struck, Paul said to the centurion, "Excuse me, but is it legal for you to punish a Roman citizen who hasn't yet been tried in a proper court of law?"

The officer was shocked. And frightened.

You see, in the lands the Romans had conquered

the Roman soldiers could do just about anything they wanted to the people living there. But actual Roman citizens had rights. They had to be properly brought before proper Roman courts and properly convicted before they could be punished.

And Paul was a Roman citizen.

So the officer put down the whip and ran to see the tribune.

"Sir," he said, "did you know that this Paul fellow was a Roman citizen?"

"No!" the tribune exclaimed. "I did not!"

And he rushed off to have a word with Paul.

"Is it true?" he asked Paul. "Are you really a Roman citizen?"

"I am," Paul nodded. "And a citizen by birth, at that."

"Why, you're a more genuine Roman than I am!" said the tribune. "I had to buy my citizenship."

And now the tribune was worried too. For he'd ordered Paul to be tied up, and even that went against the laws of Rome.

"Remove this man's chains!" he ordered his soldiers. "Immediately!"

But the tribune still had a problem. He was no closer to understanding why the Jews hated Paul. And if he couldn't work that out, then he would struggle to keep the peace.

So, the next day, he escorted Paul, unbound, before the chief priests and the Jewish council.

"My brothers," Paul began, for they were his brothers – Jews, just like him, even though they did not follow Jesus. "My brothers, I have, throughout the whole of my life, tried my very best to do what God has asked of me."

And as soon as Paul said that, the high priest, Ananias, ordered one of the men standing near Paul to punch him in the mouth!

Wiping the blood from his lip, Paul turned to Ananias and said, "God is going to punch you, you hypocrite. You accuse me of breaking our religious laws. Well, that very same law forbids what you have just done!"

"Show some respect!" the others shouted back at him. "That's the High Priest you're talking to!"

"I'm sorry," Paul replied. "I didn't realize. For our law also says that we should not speak evil of our rulers."

And that's when Paul had an idea – an idea that might just possibly take the focus off him – and prevent another punch in the mouth.

You see, some of the council members were Pharisees, just like Paul, while others belonged to a different Jewish group, the Sadducees. And those two groups did not always get along.

As I said, the Pharisees believed in the resurrection, and in the existence of spirits and angels. The Sadducees, however, did not believe in any of those things.

So Paul addressed the council again.

"I'm a Pharisee," he said. "I believe what every Pharisee, here, believes. So it seems to me that I am on trial today simply because I tell people about the resurrection from the dead."

As soon as Paul had said that, one of the Pharisees jumped up to defend their point of view.

"What if God really has spoken to this man, somehow?" he said. "What if he is operating under those instructions? If that is the case then we dare not oppose him. And, therefore, we find that he has done nothing wrong!"

The Sadducees, of course, thought this was ridiculous, and they began to argue with the Pharisees. The argument turned into a shouting match. The shouting

match turned violent. And soon everyone was punching everybody else in the mouth!

This was exactly what the tribune had not wanted. So he ordered his men to pull Paul out of the melee and escort him back to the barracks.

And, the following night, God did, indeed, speak to Paul (just like that Pharisee had suggested!).

"Don't be afraid," God told him. "You told people about me in Jerusalem. And, I promise, you will get the chance to do the same thing in Rome."

Bringing up the resurrection of the dead was a clever tactic, of course. It didn't mean that the charges against Paul would be dismissed. But the Romans, who would have to make the official decisions about Paul's guilt, learned something from this. It was now clear that the charges against Paul were religious and were not very easily resolved.

But Paul wasn't just being clever. He was being truthful. He was who he was because of Jesus' victory over death. He wrote:

"'Hey Death, you thought you won, didn't you? Hey Death, you thought you could hurt us, didn't you?'... But we give thanks to God! We win! Through our Lord Jesus Christ, God has taken care of it all. Therefore, dear brothers and sisters, stand your ground. Don't let anything shake you. Always give yourself fully to the work of the Lord. You know that your work for him is not wasted."

(1 CORINTHIANS 15:55, 57-58. SEE HOSEA 13:14)

And you know, Paul didn't let anything or anyone shake him, though plenty tried, as you'll soon see.

CHAPTER 19

GUILTY OR FREE?

ACTS 24:1 – 26:32 ▣ ROMANS 8:1–2, 5, 7, 9, 18–21

It seemed like Paul was always in trouble with someone.
Yet even when he was in trouble with everyone, Paul
knew God was with him. Even when he appeared in
law courts before judges who could find him innocent
or guilty, he didn't give up. He wrote to the believers in
Rome:

"There is no longer any 'guilty' verdict for
those who belong to Christ Jesus. Because
of him, the new law of the Spirit of life set
me free from the old law of sin and death...
Those who still live their lives their own
selfish way are always thinking of selfish
things. But those who live their life following
the Spirit always think about what the Spirit
wants... The sinful mind is against God. It
doesn't do what God's law says — it just
can't... But you are not controlled by the

> sinful. Instead, if the Spirit of God lives
> in you, you're now controlled by the Spirit.
> And if anyone does not have this Spirit of
> Christ, he doesn't really belong to Christ."
>
> (ROMANS 8:1-2, 5, 7, 9)

And there was a time when Paul had to answer to judge after judge.

Paul was safe, for the moment, locked away in the Roman barracks in Jerusalem. But the Jews who opposed him had other plans.

"Send for Paul, again," they said to the council. "And when the tribune brings him out, we will ambush them, grab hold of Paul, and kill him. There are forty of us who have vowed to let no food touch our lips until that blasphemer is dead!"

Fortunately, Paul's nephew got wind of the plot and went to tell the tribune.

"I need an armed escort," the tribune ordered his officers. "Two hundred soldiers. Seventy men on horses. And two hundred men with spears. There is a plot to kill Paul. So we are going to take him from Jerusalem to Caesarea and place him directly in the hands of Felix, the Roman governor there."

That's what they did. Paul arrived safely in Caesarea. And I suppose that the men who'd vowed not to eat until they'd killed him finished up very, very hungry indeed!

Five days later, the high priest Ananias travelled to Caesarea, accompanied by several elders and his spokesman, Tertullus, to present the case against Paul to Governor Felix.

"Most excellent Felix," Tertullus began (flattering the governor), "you have brought peace and prosperity to our land. And for that, we thank you.

"But this Paul, in contrast, has brought our people nothing but trouble. In simple terms, he is a plague on our land. He starts riots. He is a leader of the religious sect who follow Jesus. And he has even tried to bring shame upon our temple. Talk to him and you will see that everything we say is true."

So Felix gave Paul a chance to defend himself.

"You have been an excellent ruler over our people for many years," Paul began (using some flattery of his own!), "so I am happy to offer my defence.

"Check for yourself. I was in Jerusalem for only twelve days. And in that time I did nothing to stir up anyone – not in the Temple, or the synagogues, or out on the streets. As for their other charges, there is not one of them that they can prove.

"I am a follower of Jesus, yes – or the Way, as some call it. But far from being a sect, as they have suggested, I believe it is the fulfilment of all that God has tried to do among his people, from our fathers until now. It's there in our Law. It was echoed by our prophets. It's the hope of resurrection, which these men believe, as well. And I say that without shame.

"There I was, in the Temple, in the midst of a ritual of purification, when some Jews from Asia Minor – who, by rights, ought to be here with me now – began to make trouble.

"And all I said, when they brought me before the council, was that I was only there because I believed in the resurrection. That's all I did. And if there's any crime in that, or anything else I have done, then I challenge these men to lay it before you."

As it happened, Felix knew something about the followers of Jesus, and he was actually quite interested in what Paul had to say. So he told the High Priest that he was going to delay his decision until such a time as the tribune could be there too.

Then he set up a kind of house arrest for Paul, within the barracks in Caesarea, so that Paul would be protected from his enemies, but still able to see his friends and family.

During that time, Felix and his wife Drusilla, who was Jewish, listened to all that Paul had to say about Jesus. But when Paul talked about God's judgment against those who did not believe, Felix was upset and sent Paul back to his quarters.

"We'll talk about this, at some other time," he told Paul. But that "some other time" never came. And Paul

had to stay there for two whole years, until Felix was replaced by another governor, Festus.

And guess, what? The Jewish leaders tried it on again!

While Festus was in Jerusalem on a visit, they presented their case against Paul to him. They then suggested that he bring Paul from Caesarea up to Jerusalem so he could give his side of the story.

And once again they planned to ambush the convoy, along the way, and kill Paul. Talk about a lack of imagination!

Festus told them that Paul would be staying in Caesarea and that if they wanted to bring their charges against Paul, they were welcome to go down there.

Ten days later, the Jewish leaders trooped into Caesarea. And things went exactly as they had gone with the previous governor, Felix. The Jewish leaders made the same charges. Paul offered the same defence. And, in the end, they got nowhere.

Festus could see that the Jewish leaders really wanted to have their way with Paul. And he was in charge of keeping the peace. So he decided to do them a favour.

"Why don't we just go up to Jerusalem?" he suggested to Paul. "And we can hold the trial there?"

Paul wasn't foolish. He knew there was no way he would get a fair trial in Jerusalem, assuming, of course, that he made it that far alive.

However in Rome, far away from the politics of Jerusalem, the influence of the Jewish leadership, and the easily swayed mob, he had a chance. He was, after all, a Roman citizen.

And so he did what every Roman citizen had the right to do.

"I appeal to Caesar," he told Festus. "I want to take my case before the emperor and be tried in Rome."

"Right then," Festus nodded. "You have appealed to Caesar, so off to Caesar you shall go."

The Jewish leaders grumbled and moaned. Once again, their prey had escaped.

Festus wiped his forehead, relieved. This awkward situation was now in someone else's hands.

And Paul remembered God's promise. "You will be a witness to me – in Rome."

Paul must have been a little scared. He must have been a little worried. But he trusted God and he trusted Jesus. He knew that God was bringing about something new and wonderful. Again, to the Romans, he wrote:

"When I think about it, the things that are painful to us now are really nothing compared to the glory that will be shown in us. The universe God created can hardly wait for God's children to be revealed. This universe has been unable to really get going. This wasn't its own choice, but the plan of the one who controlled it. But all along there was this hope that the universe will be set free from everything always going wrong. It will be brought into that wonderful freedom with God's children."

(ROMANS 8:18–21)

And so it was that through all these trials, Paul got an all-expenses-paid trip to a place he'd long wanted to travel to: Rome. He might have preferred not going there in chains, under arrest, though.

CHAPTER 20

STORMS AND DANGER

ACTS 27:1–26 ▣ 2 CORINTHIANS 4:7–11, 16–18

In those days, sea voyages were dangerous! So when Paul went off to Rome for his trial, he was not only risking his life in court, but on the sea as well. Perhaps aware of this, he once wrote to the Corinthians:

"It's as if we have wonderful treasure. But we have it in containers that could break so easily. That's what it's like to have such outstanding capabilities — that comes from God and not ourselves. We are pushed around on every side, but we're not crushed. We are stuck for answers but don't give up. We get in trouble with people, but God doesn't leave us. We are hurt, but not destroyed. It's as though we carry around a bit of the death of Jesus in our lives. But that is in order that the life of Jesus will

> also show up in our lives. We are alive, but
> we're always in danger of dying for Jesus, so
> that his life can show up in our limited lives."
>
> (2 CORINTHIANS 4:7-11)

Well, what about that fragile container on the high and stormy seas?

As I've said, in Paul's day sailing was not the safest form of transportation. Ships tended to hug the shoreline so they could keep in sight of land. And that is why, when Paul finally set sail for Rome, he was put on a ship that stopped at ports here and there along the coast.

Paul was still a Roman prisoner, of course, and still in chains. So, along with several other prisoners, he was put under the watchful eye of a centurion called Julius.

Julius was kind to Paul. In fact, when the ship docked at Sidon, he even let Paul go ashore and visit friends who lived there.

From port to port, the ship went. And when the ship finally took a course that veered away from Italy, Julius transferred his prisoners to another ship. A ship set for Rome.

The ships were sailing ships, of course. They were totally dependent on the wind. And, as it happened, the wind was not with them on the next leg of their journey. So it took much longer to get to the island of

Crete than they expected. They finished up in a small port in a place called Fair Havens.

It sounded like a nice place to stay, and that is exactly what Paul suggested.

"Gentlemen," he said to the owner of the ship, and the captain, and the centurion. "Because our journey was delayed by the winds, we have come to that time of year when sailing becomes even more dangerous. I suggest we stay here. Otherwise, I fear that our ship will be wrecked, and many lives and cargo lost."

Paul had travelled a lot. He knew what he was talking about. But the centurion didn't know that. And even though he was kindly disposed towards Paul, the centurion was going to take the advice of an experienced sea captain every time.

"I don't think so," said the sea captain. "This harbour's too shallow a place to spend the winter. I say we sail to the other end of the island, to the port of Phoenix, and wait out the winter there."

The centurion and the owner of the ship agreed, so off they went.

The weather was fine, at first. Gentle breezes pushed them silently along the south coast of the island.

But then, the sky grew dark, the wind blew hard, and the waves rose and rolled around them. Unable to sail into the wind, they were forced to let it take them where it would.

And where it took them was out to sea, far from the sight of any safe harbour.

The sailors tried everything they could to control the ship, but the storm was just too powerful. In the end, they had to throw the ship's cargo and equipment overboard, just to keep from sinking. And still the storm did not let up.

Dark nights followed dark days as the ship was driven farther and farther out to sea. Finally, windswept and storm-tossed, exhausted and frightened and hungry, the crew gave up any hope of being saved.

And that's when Paul stood up and addressed his shipmates.

"I told you it was the wrong time of year to sail, but you did not trust me," he said, which, to be fair, was probably not the most tactful way to begin his speech. But Paul had a reason for saying that. For he was about to tell them something else. Something even more incredible. Something he hoped they would believe, this time.

"Tonight," Paul said. "Here on this very ship, I was visited by an angel – a messenger of the God I worship and serve.

"The angel told me not to be afraid.

"The angel told me that I would, indeed, reach Rome, and stand before Caesar.

"And the angel told me that not one life on this ship would be lost.

"So take heart, men. For we will all be saved."

This seemed impossible to the sailors. Too good to be true. But Paul had been right before. So perhaps he would be right once more. Their spirits began to lift. They chatted and smiled, relieved.

"Oh, and one more thing," Paul added. "The angel says that there is going to be shipwreck."

What enabled Paul to be so brave in the middle of such danger? You know the answer, don't you? He wrote of it to the Corinthians:

"We don't give up hope. On the surface, things get worse and worse. But inside, we are made new every day. The troubles and annoyances we go through are really helping us get an eternal glory. That glory is worth so much more than the troubles. So we focus our attention on the things we can't actually see, not what we can see. That's because what we see on the surface is temporary, while there are things we can't see that last forever."

(2 CORINTHIANS 4:16-18)

And speaking of "things getting worse and worse on the surface", the whole sailing ship was about to go under!

CHAPTER 21

SHIPWRECKED!

ACTS 27:27 – 28:10 ▪ COLOSSIANS 1:16C–24

The God that Paul trusted was the same God who long ago parted the sea to make the way safe for Moses. And he trusted in the Lord Jesus who could walk on water and still the storms. A shipwreck is a terrifying thing, but for Paul, Jesus was greater than anything else. He wrote this to the Colossians:

"Everything was created by Jesus and for Jesus. He was there before anything else, and he holds everything together. And Jesus is like the head of the church, which is like a body. Jesus is the beginning and first to be raised from the dead. This shows that in everything, Jesus is at the top. It made God happy to have the fullness of God live in Jesus, and through Jesus to make everything right with him.

> *That includes things on earth and in heaven.*
> *Peace was made when Jesus' blood was given*
> *on the cross."*
>
> (COLOSSIANS 1:16c-20)

Thinking like this, Paul could face anything.

For fourteen days the ship sailed through the storm, across the Adriatic, out in the open sea.

But on that fourteenth night, the sailors thought they were coming near land. So they sounded the depth of the ocean, and sure enough, the farther they went the more shallow the water became.

They had no idea where they were. But afraid that they might strike some rocky shore, they lowered a small boat from the back of the ship.

"We'll just climb into this small boat," the sailors explained. "It will make it easier to... umm... set out the anchors."

Paul could see what they were up to.

"The sailors are trying to escape," he told the centurion, knowing full well that everyone else on the ship would need their skill to get to shore. "Unless they stay on the ship with us," he went on, "you will surely die."

So the centurion ordered his soldiers to cut the ropes to the boat before the sailors could climb in. And the small boat dropped harmlessly into the sea.

As dawn approached the next morning, Paul addressed everyone on board – 276 people in all.

"We haven't eaten for two weeks," he said. "Remember, God promised that no one is going to die, but we will need all our strength for what lies ahead. So I say that we eat something. Right here, right now."

And, having said that, he took some bread and thanked God for it, and broke it, and ate it. And everyone else did the same.

Then they did what they could to lighten the ship even more. And waited for day.

When the sun rose, they could see land before them. But it was a beach that no one recognized.

So they cut the anchors free, and raised one of the sails, and let the wind drive them towards the land. Before they reached the beach, however, the ship struck a reef. The prow of the ship jammed into the rocks, while the stern was torn to pieces by the waves.

Everyone did what they could to escape to shore.

However, the soldiers guarding Paul and the other prisoners were worried. Roman law was clear. If one of those prisoners ran off, then the soldiers guarding them would receive their punishment. So the soldiers decided to do the simple thing: put the prisoners to death.

But Julius the centurion was keen to save Paul. So he foiled his soldier's plan and ordered them all – soldier and prisoner alike – into the sea.

"If you can swim," he said. "Do so. And if not, grab

onto a piece of wood from the ship and float to shore."

And so it was, that just as God promised, everyone survived.

When the people who lived on the island saw the shipwreck, they came to offer help and support. They told Paul and the others the island was called Malta.

They were incredibly helpful, and as rain had begun to fall, they gathered sticks and built a fire. Paul picked

up a bundle of sticks to throw onto the blaze. But, as he did, a snake, hiding among the sticks, leapt out and bit him on the hand.

"Oh dear," muttered one of the islanders to another. "That prisoner must be a murderer. He escaped the sea, but justice has decided that he still must die." But Paul just shook his hand and the snake fell off into the fire. And as time passed, he neither swelled up nor fell down dead.

"I think you might be wrong," said the second islander to the first. "In fact, I think that man might just be a god!"

Eventually, they were all taken to meet Publius, the governor of Malta. For three days, he fed them and housed them and cared for them. And when his father fell ill with a fever, Paul prayed for him, and the fever went away.

After this, anyone on the island who was ill came to Paul. And they were all healed. So, day by day, the respect the islanders had for Paul and for the others grew and grew and grew.

But finally, when the winter had passed, it was time. Time to set off, once again, for Rome.

Shipwrecked but alive, Paul, as ever, shared the good news of Jesus with the people he met. And when he did, he'd say something like what he wrote to the Colossians:

"You used to be far away from God. Because of your bad way of living, you thought like God's enemies. But now, God has repaired your relationship. The actual death of Christ enabled you to be presented to God as holy, without anything wrong, or anyone saying you did wrong. And this is so as long as you continue in your faith, sure and certain, staying with the hope held out to you in the message of Jesus. This is the good news that you heard. It has been passed on to every creature under heaven. And I, Paul, have become a servant of this good news of Jesus. And now I can be happy about any pain I went through for you."

(COLOSSIANS 1:21–24)

It was beginning to look as though nothing could prevent Paul from getting to Rome. What a journey!

CHAPTER 22

ROME, AT LAST

ACTS 28:17–31 ▦ ROMANS 28, 33–35, 37–39

Paul had wanted to visit Rome to share the good news about Jesus there. He can't have expected his wish to be fulfilled by arriving in chains as a prisoner and a bit bedraggled from the shipwreck. But as he had written to the Romans earlier:

"We know that in all things God works for the good of those who love him. They are people who he chose to call to himself... And who can say anything bad about the people he has chosen? Nobody — it is God who gets to say what is right. There is no one else who can accuse. Christ Jesus, who died and was raised from the dead, now sits right next to God, speaking up for us. And no one can cut us off from the love of Christ. It's there even if we have trouble, difficult times, or if people are angry with us. It's there even *if we're without food or clothes. It's there even if we're in danger or are threatened... Despite all these things, we win! That's because Jesus loves us."*

(ROMANS 8:28, 33–35, 37)

Paul must have been encouraged whenever he reflected on these words. Another encouragement was when, at last, the final part of his journey to Rome began.

Paul stayed on Malta for three months, until the winter storms were over. Then he boarded a ship from Alexandria, in Egypt, which made its way along the coast to Syracuse, then to Rhegium, on the mainland, and finally north to the port at Puteoli.

He travelled by land from there. And the promise that God had made him finally came true. He was in Rome – capital of the entire empire!

Paul was still a prisoner, of course. But a prisoner with quite a bit of freedom. He was allowed to rent his own house. He was allowed to have visitors. But he had to stay in the house, with a Roman soldier guarding him at all times.

Paul wasted no time. God had brought him safely to Rome, so he was going to take every opportunity to tell the people there about Jesus.

Three days after he arrived, he did what he had always done in the cities he'd visited. He went to the

Jews, first of all. Except, of course, he couldn't actually go anywhere, much less to the local synagogue. So he invited the leaders of the Jewish community in Rome to come to his house!

"First of all," Paul said to them, "you might have heard some unpleasant things about me, from the leaders in Jerusalem. So I want to assure you that I haven't done anything against our laws or our traditions, much less anything worthy of the death penalty.

"I'm only here in Rome, appealing my case to Caesar, because the Jewish leaders in Jerusalem would not accept the verdict of the Roman governor - who was very happy to set me free.

"In any case, I am happy to be here, because it gives me the chance to tell you about what God has done to make the hopes and dreams of our people come true."

The Jews looked at Paul curiously. And then they answered.

"Actually," they said. "We haven't heard anything about you, at all - good or bad. No letters. No visitors. Nothing.

"But we are interested in hearing what you have to say, because we have heard a lot of bad things about this Jesus sect you belong to."

Perhaps it wasn't the best opportunity, but Paul saw it as his chance. So they set a date, and when the time came, a huge number of Jews arrived at Paul's house to hear about Jesus.

He spoke from morning till evening. And, scripture passage by scripture passage, he showed them that Jesus was God's fulfilment of everything they knew from the Law of Moses and the Prophets.

Some believed what he said. Some didn't. But the biggest disagreement arose when Paul quoted a passage from the prophet Isaiah. "My own people refuse to hear me," the passage said. "They choose not to understand. So I will tell the Gentiles about my saving love. And they will listen to what I have to say."

Much as Paul had found in other places, many Jews didn't like the idea of God extending his love to the Gentiles. So, after they had argued for a while about this, his listeners got up and left.

Did that stop Paul telling other people about Jesus? Of course not! That was why God had brought him to Rome.

And so, for two years, he stayed in that house, talking about Jesus and the kingdom of God with all who would listen.

He spoke boldly. He spoke freely. And he never gave up. For he was, after all, a man on a mission!

Even under house-arrest, Paul still regarded himself as free. Nothing could stop his connection to God, as he wrote:

"Here's something I'm sure about: There is nothing that can separate us from the love of God that comes in Christ Jesus our Lord. Not death or life, not angels or demons, not the present or the future, not power, not height or depth — no thing, nowhere, no time."

(ROMANS 8:38-39)

That's how he had described his thinking to the Romans all those years ago.

But his upcoming trial in Rome wasn't the end of Paul, even though it is the end of what Luke wrote in the book of Acts. I have another letter from Paul, in which he wrote about this trial. I'll let him have the last word:

"The first time I defended myself, there was no one with me, everyone left me. Don't hold it against them. But the Lord was right there with me and gave me strength. Because of that, his news could be told and all the Gentiles could hear it through me. And I was saved from judgment. The Lord will rescue me from every evil attack. He will bring me safely to his heavenly kingdom. To him be glory for ever and ever. Amen."

(2 TIMOTHY 4:16-18)

ALSO BY BOB HARTMAN

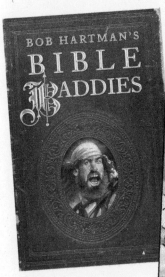

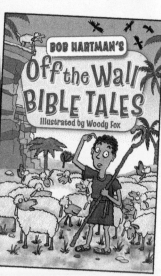

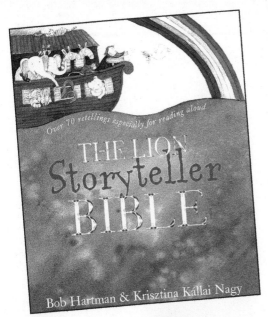

Over 70 retellings especially for reading aloud

THE LION
Storyteller
BIBLE

Bob Hartman & Krisztina Kállai Nagy

Look out for
Bob Hartman's
stories in
ebook

THE LION
Storyteller
AWESOME
BOOK OF STORIES

A collection of Bob Hartman's best stories
especially for reading aloud"

Bob Hartman & Krisztina Kállai Nagy